Formal Methods:
Theory and Practice

Formal Methods:
Theory and Practice

Edited by

P. N. Scharbach
BP Research

BSP PROFESSIONAL BOOKS
OXFORD   LONDON   EDINBURGH
BOSTON   MELBOURNE

First published 1989

British Library
Cataloguing in Publication Data

Formal methods: theory and practice.
  1. Computer systems, Programming.
  Applications of mathematical logic
  I. Scharbach, P. N.
  005.13'1.
ISBN 0–632–01931–X

BSP Professional Books
A division of Blackwell Scientific
  Publications Ltd
Editorial Offices:
Osney Mead, Oxford OX2 0EL
  (Orders: Tel. 0865 240201)
8 John Street, London WC1N 2ES
23 Ainslie Place, Edinburgh EH3 6AJ
3 Cambridge Center, Suite 208,
  Cambridge, MA 02142, USA
107 Barry Street, Carlton, Victoria 3053,
  Australia

Set by Computate (Pickering) Ltd

Printed and bound in Great Britain by
Mackays of Chatham PLC, Chatham, Kent

Contents

Contributors' Biographies

S. King is a Research Officer at the Programming Research Group, Oxford University, engaged on the application of formal methods to the IBM Customer Information Control System CICS. (*Chapter 4*)

Dr Li Da-Hai completed his PhD in the Department of Computing at Imperial College, London, and is now at the University of Peking. (*Chapter 3*)

Dr T. S. E. Maibaum is a Reader in Computing Science at Imperial College, London. He is the author, with Professor W. Turski, of *The Specification of Computer Programs* (Addison-Wesley, 1987.) (*Chapter 3*)

Dr P. N. Scharbach is a Computer Scientist in the Software Engineering Section, Information Technology Research Unit, BP Research Centre, Sunbury-on-Thames, England. He is a member of the Committee of the British Computer Society Formal Aspects of Computing Science Group. (*Chapter 1*)

Dr I. H. Sørensen is a University Lecturer in Computation and Industrial Liaison Officer at the Programming Research Group, Oxford University. He is also Leader, Software Engineering Section, Information Technology Research Unit, BP Research Centre. (*Chapter 4*)

A. J. Tocher is a Principal Software Engineer at STC Technology Ltd, Newcastle-under-Lyme, England, currently under secondment as consultant in formal methods to the Advanced Networked Systems Architecture Project, Cambridge. (*Chapter 2*)

Dr J. C. P. Woodcock is an Atlas-Rutherford Research Fellow at the Programming Research Group, Oxford and consultant to the Oxford-IBM CICS Project. He is the author, with M. Loomes, of *Software Engineering Mathematics* (Pitman, 1988). (*Chapter 5*)

Foreword

The purpose of this book is to illustrate the use of formal system theories and notations in a spectrum of practical applications. The aspects of system specification, development and verification are covered, using realistic examples. The formal methods employed are sufficiently mature (in one case approaching international standardisation) that basic tutorial material is not included if readily accessible elsewhere.

It is hoped that the reader will gain insight into the practice of formal methods as well as motivation for further study of their theoretical foundations.

P. N. Scharbach

Chapter 1

Formal Methods: Theory and Practice

P. N. SCHARBACH

Formal methods have long been developed and advocated within the computing science research community as providing a sound mathematical foundation for the specification, implementation and verification of computer systems. These methods exploit representations with formally defined semantics in order to describe abstractly, and independently of details of implementation, the desired functional behaviour of a system to be developed [Berg *et al.*, 1982; Cohen *et al.*, 1986]. Such descriptions provide precise, unambiguous system specifications which can be checked for completeness and internal logical consistency. The mathematical nature of these specifications enables *reasoning* about consistency (is the specified system dynamics consistent with the system's static properties?) and the deduction of consequences of the specification. These can be checked against the user's expectations and used to generate tests for the final system implementation.

Specifications in a formal language which is executable, or possesses an executable subset, provide direct simulations (*animations*) of system behaviour, giving early feedback to be compared with user requirements before full system development is begun. Equally important in the system development process, a formal specification is a yardstick against which to *verify* implementations or implementation steps through mathematical proof of the equivalence of abstract and concrete representations of system operations or data structures [Jones, 1986].

Nevertheless it is only in the past few years that formal methods have begun to be applied seriously on industrial projects. There are several reasons for this and they involve a certain degree of circularity. Small example applications, such as stacks and the alternating bit protocol, have been formally specified and analysed repeatedly. But it is only quite recently that a body of experience has been accumulating in the application of these methods to industrial-scale problems. It has therefore been difficult to assess the practical benefits and economics of the use of formal methods. Undeniably, their adoption has significant consequences for the planning and management of system development.

A formally based development methodology requires in effect that a mathematical theory of the desired system be created, documented and analysed. This foundational activity entails a greater proportion of time and effort being invested in the initial, pre-design, phases of system development than is now commonly the case. We believe that, thanks to the rigorous discipline imposed by these methods, later system development phases will be rendered less error-prone, more systematic and amenable to computer assistance, and hence higher quality products achieved. But project managers are naturally reluctant to adopt new methods in the absence of a substantial base of experience in the ramifications of their use.

A related concern is the 'maturity' of a formal method under consideration for adoption. Has the method been tested against real problems or only against straw men? Is the formalism sufficiently stable that it can be standardised, and support tools built? Do accessible texts and training courses exist for the method?

Throughout the above discussion, the term 'system' has been used without differentiation between software and hardware systems. It is, however, the application of formal methods to software systems that is illustrated in this book. Although the exploration of formalisms suitable for hardware specification and verification is an expanding area of research (see, e.g., [Hunt, 1985; Milne and Subrahmanyam, 1986]), techniques and tools are at an early experimental stage and few realistic case studies have been performed.

A significant recent achievement is the formal specification of the functionality of VIPER, a 32-bit microprocessor designed specifically for safety-critical control applications. (VIPER is a registered trade mark of the UK Ministry of Defence.) In view of the serious consequences of VIPER malfunctioning the usual approach of testing for fault detection was inadequate, and the VIPER gate-level logic design was successfully verified to conform to the high-level formal specification [Cohn, 1987]. The development and application of formal methods for hardware design can be expected to expand with the trend to install microprocessors in safety-critical roles such as protection systems.

This book is intended to provide an introduction to the application of formal methods for ensuring the reliable development and maintenance of software systems. A number of techniques and applications are demonstrated here, selected for the relative maturity of the methods and the interest of the application. Each technique discussed is illustrated by a non-trivial application. Formal techniques appropriate to sequential and concurrent systems are demonstrated. Example applications are drawn from the areas of transaction processing, distributed systems and communications protocols.

Chapter 2 describes an application of the formal description language LOTOS [ISO, 1987] to the specification of the Open Systems Interconnection (OSI) Transport Service standard. An introduction to LOTOS, a process-based language developed by the International Standards Organisation (ISO) for the formal description of OSI service and protocol standards, is provided. The language was designed specifically to enable precise and unambiguous communications standards to be formulated and analysed. This is obviously an activity of extreme importance given the scale of investment in systems interworking. LOTOS is itself expected to become an ISO standard formal description technique. Support tools for LOTOS are being produced by the SEDOS project within the European Commission's ESPRIT information technology initiative.

Non-classical logics have been developed in order to express and formalise the concepts of time, necessity and possibility. These formalisations enlarge the scope of the nature of assertions that can be made, and verified, about system behaviour (e.g. 'The message will eventually arrive at its destination'). Such logics are a powerful tool for proving properties of concurrent systems, a notoriously subtle area [Apt, 1985]. Modal and temporal operators are used in Chapter 3 for the specification of a token-passing protocol for a ring network. The criteria for a formalism for protocol development are established, and a methodology for the systematic construction of the protocol from the specifications of the service it relies upon and the services it is intended to provide, is illustrated. A logic formalism is applied to prove the correctness of the resulting protocol.

A transaction processing example is used in Chapter 4 to illustrate the use of the model-based specification language Z and the derivation (*refinement*) of code from an abstract specification. Z has been developed at the Oxford University Programming Research Group over the past decade, and an extensive collection of case studies in its application has been documented [Hayes, 1987]. A notable feature of Z is the *schema*, introduced in order to present specifications in a modular fashion [Spivey, 1988]. Modularisation is of vital importance in the description and comprehension of large complex systems. Both the abstract state of a system (its static properties) and the operations it engages in (its dynamics) are expressed in schema notation. The notation has been used successfully in the documentation and maintenance of the IBM Customer Information Control System (CICS), an online transaction processing system consisting of over 500 000 lines of code. Chapter 4 exploits a database application to illustrate the Z formalisation of the program development process in use at IBM Hursley. Specifications in Z are refined to algorithms expressed in Dijkstra's guarded command language [Gries, 1981]. The chapter also illustrates the proof obligations generated in the verification that the code satisfies its formal specification. A summary of the IBM experience with Z is presented in [Collins *et al.*, 1987]. Z support tools (syntax and type checkers) have been produced by the FORSITE collaboration within the Alvey Programme. Industrial training courses in Z are available from several UK software houses.

Finally, the use of the specification language CSP (Communicating Sequential Processes) is illustrated on a multiple-process transaction processing system in Chapter 5. CSP is a process-based formalism for the description of concurrent systems, and possesses a rich set of mathematical laws for their analysis [Hoare, 1985]. The approach taken in Chapter 5 is to specify individual system requirements separately as assertions on traces of observable events. These are implemented by simple CSP processes. The overall system is then described by the parallel composition of these processes. The laws of CSP enable proofs that process algebra models satisfy the trace specifications. The theory of CSP (which has had a strong influence on the design of LOTOS) is given in [Hoare, 1985].

The selection of formalisms discussed in this book is representative rather than in any sense complete. In particular, the Vienna Development Method (VDM), which has seen application in several industrial contexts, is not illustrated here. Expositions of VDM may be found in [Jones, 1980; Jones, 1986].

REFERENCES

Apt, K. R. *ed.* (1985), *Logics and Models of Concurrent Systems*, Springer-Verlag.

Berg, H. E. , Boebert, W. E., Franta, W. R. and Moher, T. G. (1982), *Formal Methods of Program Verification and Specification*, Prentice-Hall Inc.

Collins, B. P., Nicholls, J. E. and Sørensen, I. H. (1987), *Introducing Formal Methods: the CICS Experience with Z*, IBM Technical Report TR12.260, IBM United Kingdom Laboratories, Hursley.

Cohen, B., Harwood, W. T. and Jackson, M. I. (1986), *The Specification of Complex Systems*, Addison-Wesley Publishing Company.

Cohn, A. J. (1987), *Proceedings of the Calgary Hardware Verification Workshop*, 'A Proof of Correctness of the VIPER Microprocessor: The First Level', Calgary, Canada.

Gries, D. (1981), *The Science of Programming*, Springer-Verlag.

Hayes, I. *ed.* (1987), *Specification Case Studies*, Prentice-Hall International.

Hoare, C. A. R. (1985), *Communicating Sequential Processes*, Prentice-Hall International.

Hunt, W. A. (1985), *FM8501: a Verified Microprocessor*, Institute of Computing Science Technical Report 47, University of Texas at Austin.

ISO DIS 8807 (1987), *Information Processing Systems – Open Systems Interconnection – LOTOS, a Formal Description Technique Based on the Temporal Ordering of Observational Behaviour*, Geneva: International Standards Organisation.

Jones, C. B. (1980), *Software Development: a Rigorous Approach*, Prentice-Hall International.

Jones, C. B. (1986), *Systematic Software Development Using VDM*, Prentice-Hall International.

Milne, G. and Subrahmanyam, P. A. *eds.* (1986), *Formal Aspects of VLSI Design*, North-Holland, 'Why Higher Order Logic is a Good Formalism for Specifying and Verifying Hardware'.

Spivey, J. M. (1988), *Introducing Z: a Specification Language and its Formal Semantics*, Cambridge University Press.

Chapter 2

LOTOS and the Formal Specification of Communication Standards: An Example

A. J. TOCHER

2.1 INTRODUCTION

In this chapter an informal introduction is given to the Language fOr Temporal Ordering Specifications (LOTOS) [DIS 8807, 1987] developed by the International Standards Organisation (ISO) for the description of Open Systems Interconnection (OSI) services and protocols. This introduction focuses on the application of LOTOS to one particular OSI service: the transport service [ISO 8072, 1984]. It is intended that the specification of the service presented here be as complete as feasible, but only those features of LOTOS necessary to understand the specification are presented. The interested reader is referred to [DIS 8807, 1987] for further details of the language.

The chapter is divided into four principal parts: an introduction to the basic theory behind LOTOS data types; the practical application of that theory to the service specification; an introduction to the specification of dynamic behaviour in LOTOS; and its application to the transport service specification.

To complete this introduction, short overviews of both LOTOS and the transport service are given, followed by some brief mathematical preliminaries.

2.1.1 LOTOS

LOTOS is a formal description language developed within ISO/TC97/ SC21/WG1, the ISO working group concerned with architectural issues for OSI. It was designed to meet the following objectives [ISO, 1984]:

(a) to allow preparation of unambiguous, clear, and precise descriptions of OSI standards;
(b) to allow verification of descriptions for consistency and correctness;

(c) to provide, for implementors and designers of OSI systems, clear guidance on what should be implemented, but not how it should be implemented;

(d) to act as a sound basis for conformance testing.

In order to achieve these objectives LOTOS has been defined on a firm mathematical basis and has its origins in two forms of algebraic specification language.

The specification of data types in LOTOS uses a variant of the algebraic abstract data type language ACT ONE [Ehrig and Mahr, 1985] using an initial algebra approach to data type definition [McLane and Birkhoff, 1979].

Specification of dynamic behaviours in LOTOS is based on process algebras. Whilst it is predominantly based on Milner's Calculus of Communicating Systems (CCS) [Milner, 1980], the treatment of parallelism and concurrency has been strongly influenced by Hoare's Communicating Sequential Processes (CSP) [Hoare, 1985] and this has had a beneficial effect on the structuring of LOTOS specifications.

2.1.2 The ISO OSI transport service

The transport service provides a communication service by means of which service users may establish, maintain, and relinquish communication connections between each other. The boundary at which the service and users interact is made up of an indeterminate, and possibly varying, number of service access points each of which is uniquely identified by a service address. Each service access point is, in turn, made up of a similarly indeterminate, and possibly varying, number of connection endpoints, each uniquely identified, within the access point, by an endpoint identifier. Any endpoint may therefore be uniquely identified by the combination of its address and its endpoint identifier.

Connections are established between named addresses. The endpoint identifiers are allocated locally within each access point, and serve only to distinguish multiple connections using the same address. The messages communicated at the endpoints are known as *service primitives*. The precise nature of these primitives is described later.

2.1.3 Some mathematical preliminaries

The exposition of LOTOS given here is based on the notions of axioms, derivation rules, and derivations.

A derivation rule is an assertion of the form

$$\frac{P_1, \ldots, P_n}{P}$$

where $P_1, \ldots, P_n$ are propositions. Informally, it is interpreted as meaning that if each of the P_is is a valid proposition, then so is P. That is, the validity of P may be *derived* from that of the P_is.

Such a rule presupposes that it is possible to derive the validity of the P_is by some means. To make this possible it is necessary to have at least one proposition which can be shown to be valid without requiring prior derivation of the validity of another proposition. Such a proposition is known as an *axiom*. An axiom is a proposition which is stated to be valid in its own right.

A derivation of a proposition, P_n, is defined as a finite sequence of propositions, $P_i(i\colon 1 \ldots n)$ such that each P_i either is an axiom, or can be derived from the preceding P_is by the application of a single derivation rule.

For a given set of axioms and derivation rules, a proposition P is deemed to be valid if and only if it has a derivation based on those axioms and rules.

2.2 DATA TYPES IN THEORY

2.2.1 Simple data types

Data type definitions in LOTOS have four principal components: a type name, declarations of a set of sort names and of a set of operation signatures, and a set of algebraic equations.

The *type name* denotes the algebra formed from the sorts, operations, and equations given in the type definition.

The *sort names* of a data type denote the sets of values (sorts) which are defined in the type, and are used in defining the domain and range of the operations. The nature of the values associated with a given name is determined by the operations and the equations.

The *operation signatures* define the functionality of the operations: the sorts of the operators' arguments and the sorts of their result. It is possible for an operation to have no arguments, in which case it may be thought of as a constant of its result sort. For example, if *BOOL* denotes the Boolean sort, then the signature

```
true,
false  : - > BOOL
```

declares *true* and *false* to be constants of sort *BOOL*. The signatures

```
not  : BOOL - > BOOL
_or_ : BOOL, BOOL - > BOOL
```

declare *not* and *or* to be operations from a single Boolean to a Boolean, and from a pair of Booleans to a Boolean respectively.

An important aspect of the operations defined is that they must denote total functions; they must be defined for all values of their domain sorts. It will be seen in the service specification that certain potential problems arise because of an apparent need to define and use non-total operations. However a means to overcome this is shown.

By default, operations are defined to be prefix, but surrounding the operator name in the signature by underscores, '_', defines the operator to be infix. Only expressions constructed using the operations may be used to denote values of the defined sorts. For example if b_1 and b_2 are expressions of sort *BOOL*, then the following are all valid expressions of sort *BOOL*:

> true
> false
> not (b_1)
> b_1 or b_2

The equations of a type definition define which expressions of the type denote the same value. Evidently in the case of *BOOL* each expression should be equivalent to *true* or *false*, if it is to match the intuitive understanding of the Boolean type. This can be expressed in the following equations where b denotes an arbitrary expression of sort BOOL:

> not (true) = false;
> not (false) = true;
>
> true or b = true;
> false or b = b

These equations form the axioms of a derivation system for proving expressions to be equivalent. Two implicit derivation rules complete the derivation system. The first of these states that equivalence is commutative:

$$\frac{E_1 = E_2}{E_2 = E_1}$$

whilst the second states the law of substitution: if two expressions are equivalent, then one may be substituted for the other in any other expression:

$$\frac{E_1 = E_2, E_3 = E_4}{([E_2/E_1]E_3) = E_4}$$

where $[E_2/E_1]E_3$ denotes the textual substitution of E_2 for all occurrences of E_1 in E_3.

Two expressions, E_1 and E_2, are deemed to denote the same value if and only if $E_1 = E_2$ can be derived from the equations and the derivation rules.

This approach, of assuming all expressions to denote distinct values unless stated to denote the same value, characterises the initial algebra approach to semantics. The technical details of this approach are not further expounded here, but the interested reader is referred to [MacLane and Birkhoff, 1979] for an abstract approach to the topic, or to [Ehrig and Mahr, 1985] for a more practical introduction, including the definition of the ACT ONE language on which the LOTOS type definitions are based.

Collecting all the type definition components together gives the type definition *BOOLEANtype*. Place holders for expressions, such as the *b* in the equations, must be declared prior to their use, and are to be found in the **forall** clause of the definition.

```
type  BOOLEANtype
is
sorts
        BOOL
opns
        true,
        false      : -> BOOL

        not        : BOOL -> BOOL
        _or_       : BOOL, BOOL -> BOOL
eqns
forall
        b          : BOOL
ofsort  BOOL
        not (true)  = false;
        not (false) = true;

        true or b   = true;
        false or b  = b
endtype (* BOOLEANtype *)
```

2.2.2 Enriching data types

Given a type definition, it is possible to enrich it by adding further sort and operation definitions. This is achieved by defining a new type to include a previous type definition, as in the case of type *BOOLtype*, which through its reference to *BOOLEANtype* inherits all the definitions embodied in that type. So *BOOLtype* defines the same sort and operations as *BOOLEANtype*, but also enriches them with the addition of two further operations, *and* and = = > (logical implication).

Type *BOOLtype* is very similar to a data type, *Bool*, which is defined as part of a standard library of LOTOS data types in an annexe of [DIS 8807, 1987]. For the purposes of the application which follows the two will be assumed to be identical.

```
type  BOOLtype
is
        BOOLEANtype
with
opns
        _and_,
        _ = = >_   : BOOL, BOOL -> BOOL
eqns
forall
```

        b1, b2   : BOOL
ofsort BOOL
        b1 and b2   = not ((not(b1)) or (not(b2)));
        b1 = = > b2 = (not b1) or b2;
endtype (* BOOLtype *)

2.2.3   Conditional equations

It is possible in LOTOS to state equations which hold dependent on the
validity of certain other equations. These are known as conditional equations, and represent a facility to express derivation rules in LOTOS.
Conditional equations are of the form:

$$E_1 = E_2 = > E_3 = E_4$$

This is interpreted as meaning that if $E_1 = E_2$ is derivable, then so is $E_3 = E_4$.
This clearly corresponds to a derivation rule:

$$\frac{E_1 = E_2}{E_3 = E_4}$$

For example, an alternative formulation of the equivalences for $= = >$
using conditional equations is:

        b1 = true
                = >   b1 = = > b2   = b2;
        b1 = false
                = >   b1 = = > b2   = true

Evidently in this case the original formulation is shorter, but conditional
equations may in general be used as a powerful means of reducing the
number of equations required to define data types.

2.2.4   Boolean equality

It is important to note that the proof theoretic equivalence, $=$, defined by the
axioms is not the same as a Boolean operation evaluating to *true* or *false*. If
such a Boolean operation is required, then it must be explicitly defined in
each data type as required.

2.3   DATA TYPES IN PRACTICE

Having looked briefly at the theory underlying data type definition of
LOTOS, the data types employed in the specification of the transport service
may now be presented in detail.

2.3.1 Transport service primitives

The key data type on which the transport service is based is that of the transport service primitive. There are four kinds of primitive: T-CONNECT, T-DATA, T-EXPEDITED-DATA and T-DISCONNECT.

For each kind of primitive two distinct forms are identified, known as *requests* and *indications*. These classifications denote the direction in which the primitive in question is communicated at the service boundary: requests pass from the user to the service; indications pass from the service to the user. In the case of T-CONNECTs, a further two forms are permitted. These are known as *responses* and *confirmations*. Responses, like requests, are communicated from the user to the service; confirmations, like indications, go from the service to the user.

Each of the primitives is constructed from a number of component values. A T-CONNECT request is issued by a user requiring a connection to be established and contains details of that user's address (the calling address) and the address to which connection is to be made (the called address). In addition it contains details of whether the facility to send T-EXPEDITED-DATA primitives is requested, along with another component relating to the general quality of service requested (including proposed throughput, maximum transit delay, etc.). Lastly, the request may also contain some user data. A T-CONNECT indication contains all the same components, but is issued by the service at the called address, as a consequence of receiving a T-CONNECT request from the calling user.

The T-CONNECT response may be issued by a called user in response to receiving a T-CONNECT indication. The response contains details of the responding (called) user's address, but not of the calling user's address. It also contains replies to the proposals in the received T-CONNECT indication regarding acceptance of T-EXPEDITED-DATA primitives and the quality of service requested. Lastly, it may also contain user data from the called user. The confirmation contains the same components, but is issued by the service to the calling user. The response and confirmation may be considered as a form of acknowledgement to a T-CONNECT request and indication, and could have been defined as a separate kind of primitive, say 'T-CONNECT-ACKNOWLEDGE', with responses and confirmations mapped to requests and indications. Use is made of this potential simplification in the LOTOS specification.

T-DATA primitives may contain only user data, as may T-EXPEDITED-DATA primitives. Requests of either kind may be issued by the called and calling users following occurrence of a T-CONNECT response or confirmation at their respective endpoints. T-EXPEDITED-DATA primitives may also only occur if both users and the service have agreed, in the T-CONNECTs, to support this facility.

A T-DISCONNECT request may also only contain user data, but a T-DISCONNECT indication contains both user data and a reason for the issue of the indication: whether it was caused by a user or by the service provider. Following occurrence of a T-DISCONNECT at an endpoint, no further primitives may occur at that end of the associated connection. New, distinct connections may however be established which subsequently use the same endpoint identifier.

The information relating to the structure of primitives is captured in the signatures of **type** *TSPtype*, where *TA* denotes the transport address sort, *TEXOPTION* the transport expedited option selection sort, *TQOS* the quality of service sort, and *TDATA* the sort modelling user data. *TDISREASON* denotes the two-valued sort representing the reasons for disconnection. These sorts, together with the standard sort *BOOL* are all imported in the corresponding types named in the **is** clause.

For each kind of primitive a distinct constructor operation is defined which maps argument expressions to primitives. For the operation names the abbreviations used in [ISO 8072, 1984] are adopted. For example, the operator *TCONreq* constructs a T-CONNECT request primitive.

Now all of these operations introduced so far are constructors of primitives. However it is necessary to be able to determine, given an arbitrary primitive, precisely what kind of primitive it is: whether T-CONNECT, T-DATA, T-EXPEDITED-DATA, or T-DISCONNECT; and whether a request or an indication. To this end a number of testing operations are defined. These map primitives to Boolean values *true* and *false* according to whether the primitive has the required attribute or not. For example *isTCON(tsp)* is equivalent to *true* when *tsp* denotes a T-CONNECT request or indication, otherwise it is equivalent to *false*. Note the use of the operation *isTCAK* to identify whether a primitive is a T-CONNECT response or confirmation: that is, whether it is a 'T-CONNECT-ACKNOWLEDGE'. Similar operations are defined for the other kinds of primitive, and for *isTreq* and *isTind* which test whether a given primitive is a request or indication respectively. Also, compound testing operations (e.g. whether a primitive is both a T-CONNECT and a request) are defined in terms of the simpler operations. The precise equivalences required are defined in the equations of **type** *TSPtype*.

Lastly, a Boolean equality operator is defined for primitives.

    type TSPtype
    is

            BOOLtype,
            TAtype,
            TEXOPTIONtype,
            TQOStype,
            TDATAtype,
            TDISREASONtype
    with
    sorts
        TSP

opns

TCONreq,	TCONind	: TA, TA, TEXOPTION,
		TQOS, TDATA -> TSP
TCONresp,	TCONconf	: TA, TEXOPTION, TQOS,
		TDATA -> TSP
TDTreq,	TDTind	: TDATA -> TSP
TEXreq,	TEXind	: TDATA -> TSP
TDISreq		: TDATA -> TSP
TDISind		: TDISREASON, TDATA
		-> TSP

isTCONreq,	isTCONind,	isTCON,
isTCONresp,	isTCONconf,	isTCAK,
isTDTreq,	isTDTind,	isTDT,
isTEXreq,	isTEXind,	isTEX,
isTDISreq,	isTDISind,	isTDIS : TSP -> BOOL

isTreq,	isTind	: TSP -> BOOL

_ = = _   : TSP, TSP -> BOOL

eqns
forall

tsp	: TSP,
ta, ta1, ta1a	: TA,
teo	: TEXOPTION,
tq	: TQOS,
td	: TDATA,
tdr	: TDISREASON

ofsort BOOL

isTCON (TCONreq (ta1, ta1a, teo, tq, td))	= true;
isTCON (TCONind (ta1, ta1a, teo, tq, td))	= true;
isTCON (TCONresp (ta, teo, tq, td))	= false;
isTCON (TCONconf (ta, teo, tq, td))	= false;
isTCON (TDTreq (td))	= false;
isTCON (TDTind (td))	= false;
isTCON (TEXreq (td))	= false;
isTCON (TEXind (td))	= false;
isTCON (TDISreq (td))	= false;
isTCON (TDISind (tdr, td))	= false;

isTCON (tsp) = true	
= > isTCAK (tsp)	= false;
isTCAK (TCONresp (ta, teo, tq, td))	= true;
isTCAK (TCONconf (ta, teo, tq, td))	= true;
isTCAK (TDTreq (td))	= false;
isTCAK (TDTind (td))	= false;
isTCAK (TEXreq (td))	= false;

isTCAK (TEXind (td))	= false;
isTCAK (TDISreq (td))	= false;
isTCAK (TDISind (tdr, td))	= false;

(isTCON(tsp) or isTCAK(tsp)) = true
       = >   isTDT(tsp) = false;

isTDT (TDTreq (td))	= true;
isTDT (TDTind (td))	= true;
isTDT (TEXreq (td))	= false;
isTDT (TEXind (td))	= false;
isTDT (TDISreq (td))	= false;
isTDT (TDISind (tdr, td))	= false;

(isTCON(tsp) or isTCAK(tsp) or isTDT(tsp)) = true
       = >   isTEX(tsp) = false;

isTEX (TEX(td))	= true;
isTEX (TEXind (td))	= true;
isTEX (TDISreq (td))	= false;
isTEX (TDISind (tdr, td))	= false;

(isTCON(tsp) or isTCAK(tsp) or isTDT(tsp)
          or isTEX(tsp)) = true
       = >   isTDIS(tsp) = false;

isTDIS (TDISreq (td))	= true;
isTDIS (TDISind (tdr, td))	= true;

isTreq (TCONreq (ta1, ta1a, teo, tq, td))	= true;
isTreq (TCONind (ta1, ta1a, teo, tq, td))	= false;
isTreq (TCONresp (ta, teo, tq, td))	= true;
isTreq (TCONconf (ta, teo, tq, td))	= false;
isTreq (TDTreq (td))	= true;
isTreq (TDTind (td))	= false;
isTreq (TEXreq (td))	= true;
isTreq (TEXind (td))	= false;
isTreq (TDISreq (td))	= true;
isTreq (TDISind (tdr, td))	= false;

isTind(tsp)	= not (isTreq(tsp));

isTCONreq (tsp)	= isTCON(tsp) and isTreq(tsp);
isTCONind (tsp)	= isTCON(tsp) and isTind(tsp);
isTCONresp (tsp)	= isTCAK(tsp) and isTreq(tsp);
isTCONconf (tsp)	= isTCAK(tsp) and isTind(tsp);
isTDTreq (tsp)	= isTDT(tsp) and isTreq(tsp);
isTDTind (tsp)	= isTDT(tsp) and isTind(tsp);
isTEXreq (tsp)	= isTEX(tsp) and isTreq(tsp);
isTEXind (tsp)	= isTEX(tsp) and isTind(tsp);
isTDISreq (tsp)	= isTDIS(tsp) and isTreq(tsp);
isTDISind (tsp)	= isTDIS(tsp) and isTind(tsp);

TCONreq (ta1, ta1a, teo1, tq1, td1)
     = = TCONreq (ta2, ta2a, teo2, tq2, td2)
     = ((ta1 = = ta2) and (ta1a = = ta2a)
     and (teo1 = = teo2)
     and (tq1 = = tq2) and (td1 = = td2);
(isTCONreq(tsp1) and not(isTCONreq(tsp2))) = true
     = >   tsp1 = = tsp2   = false;

TCONind (ta1, ta1a, teo1, tq1, td1)
     = = TCONind (ta2, ta2a, teo2, tq2, td2)
     = ((ta1 = = ta2) and (ta1a = = ta2a)
     and (teo1 = = teo2)
     and (tq1 = = tq2) and (td1 = = td2));

(isTCONind(tsp1) and not(isTCONind(tsp2))) = true
     = >   tsp1 = = tsp2   = false;

TCONresp (ta1, teo1, tq1, td1)
     = = TCONresp (ta2, teo2, tq2, td2)
     = ((ta1 = = ta2) and (teo1 = = teo2)
     and (tq1 = = tq2) and (td1 = = td2));
(isTCONresp(tsp1)and not(isTCONresp(tsp2))) = true
     = >   tsp1 = = tsp2   = false;

TCONconf (ta1, teo1, tq1, td1)
     = = TCONconf (ta2, teo2, tq2, td2)
     = ((ta1 = = ta2) and (teo1 = = teo2)
     and (tq1 = = tq2) and (td1 = = td2);
(isTCONconf(tsp1) and not(isTCONconf(tsp2))) = true
     = >   tsp1 = = tsp2   = false;

TDTreq(td1) = = TDTreq(td2)   = td1 = = td2;
(isTDTind(tsp1) and not(isTDTreq(tsp2))) = true
     = >   tsp1 = = tsp2   = false;

TDTind (td1) = = TDTind (td2)   = td1 = = td2;
(isTDTind(tsp1) and not(isTDTind(tsp2))) = true
     = >   tsp1 = = tsp2   = false;

TEXreq (td1) = = TEXreq (td2)   = td1 = = td2;
(isTEXreq(tsp1) and not(isTEXreq(tsp2))) = true
     = >   tsp1 = = tsp2   = false;

TEXind (td1) = = TEXind (td2)   = td1 = = td2;
(isTEXind(tsp1) and not(isTEXind(tsp2))) = true
     = >   tsp1 = = tsp2   = false;

TDISreq (td1) = = TDISreq (td2)   = td1 = = td2;
(isTDISreq(tsp1) and not(isTDISreq(tsp2))) = true
     = >   tsp1 = = tsp2   = false;

TDISind (tdr1, td1) = = TDISind (tdr2, td2)
                    = (tdr1 = = tdr2) and(td1 = = td2);

(isTDISind(tsp1) and not(isTDISind(tsp2)) = true
         = >   tsp1 = = tsp2   = false

endtype (* TSPtype *)

2.3.2   Transport service primitive components

2.3.2.1   Transport service addresses
The type *TAtype* defines a set of values denoting service addresses.

The two operators, *someTA* and *anotherTA*, together define an infinite set of distinct values denoting addresses. The only relation between addresses needed in the service specification is that of Boolean equality, $= =$. This is used in the definition of equality of primitives.

type TAtype
is
        BOOLtype
with
sorts
        TA
opns
        someTA   : -> TA
        anotherTA: TA -> TA
        _ = = _   : TA, TA -> BOOL
eqns
forall
        ta1, ta2   : TA
ofsort BOOL
        someTA = = someTA   = true;
        someTA = = anotherTA(ta2)   = false;
        anotherTA(ta1) = = someTA   = false;
        anotherTA(ta1) = = anotherTA(ta2) = ta1 = = ta2;

endtype (* TAtype *)

2.3.2.2   Transport expedited data option
Type *TEXOPTION* is used to indicate whether the expedited data transfer option is requested or accepted on a given connection. The value *acceptTEX* is used to indicate that expedited data items are to be accepted, and the value *refuseTEX* that they are not.

If a calling user proposes that T-EXPEDITED-DATA primitives be permitted on a connection, it is nevertheless possible for either the service or the called user to be unable to support this facility. Either may therefore make a counter-proposal which either leaves the initial proposal unchanged, or reduces it to non-acceptance of T-EXPEDITED-DATA primitives. The operation < = is used to define the relation between proposals and counter-proposals. The expression *eo* 1 < = *eo* 2 is equivalent to *true* provided *eo* 1 does not indicate acceptance of T-EXPEDITED-DATA requests when *eo* 2 does not; otherwise it is equivalent to *false*.

Once again, a Boolean equality must be defined to support the definition of equality of primitives.

type TEXOPTIONtype
is
    BOOLEANtype
with
sorts
    TEXOPTION
opns
    acceptTEX : - > TEXOPTION
    refuseTEX : - > TEXOPTION

    _ = = _
    _ < = _   : TEXOPTION, TEXOPTION - > BOOLEAN
eqns
forall
    b1, b2   : TEXOPTION

ofsort TEXOPTION
    acceptTEX = = acceptTEX = true;
    acceptTEX = = refuseTEX = false;
    refuseTEX = = acceptTEX = false;
    refuseTEX = = refuseTEX = true;

    b1 < = b2 = (b1 = = b2) or (b1 = = refuseTEX)

endtype (* TEXOPTIONtype *)

2.3.2.3 Transport quality of service

The values of this sort are the quality of service parameters of the primitives. These are not fully defined in [ISO 8072, 1984]. However this specification is concerned only with the ordering of qualities of service: that is, what it means for one quality of service to be lower than or equal to another. Informally, if *qos* 1 and *qos* 2 are two qualities of service, then the expression *qos* 1 < = *qos* 2 should be equivalent to *true* if *qos* 1 is in some sense lower than or equal to *qos* 2, otherwise it will be equivalent to *false*.

The LOTOS specification of **type** *TQOStype* is given here only in skeletal form,'. . .' indicating where details are omitted.

Again a Boolean equality operation is necessary.

```
type  TQOStype
is
      BOOLtype,
      . . .
with
sorts
      TQOS
opns
      _ < = _,
      _ = = _     : TQOS, TQOS - > BOOLEAN
      . . .
eqns
      . . .
endtype (* TQOStype *)
```

2.3.2.4   Transport user data

This type has as its values the user data items which may be passed in primitives. Once again, the precise details of the structure of the type are omitted, other than an indication that a Boolean equality is necessary.

```
type  TDATAtype
is
      BOOLtype,
      . . .
with
sorts
      TDATA
opns
      _ = = _   : TDATA, TDATA - > BOOL
      . . .
eqns
      . . .
endtype (* TDATAtype *)
```

2.3.2.5   Transport disconnection reasons

This is the set of reasons for which a disconnect may occur. Two TS disconnect reasons are identified: disconnection caused by a user, *userTDISREASON*, and disconnection caused by the service provider, *providerTDISREASON*.

```
type  TDISREASONtype
is
sorts
      TDISREASON
opns
      userTDISREASON,
      providerTDISREASON   : - > TDISREASON
      _ = = _                 : TDISREASON, TDISREASON - > BOOL
```

eqns

userTDISREASON = = userTDISREASON	= true;
userTDISREASON = = providerTDISREASON	= false;
providerTDISREASON = = userTDISREASON	= false;
providerTDISREASON = = providerTDISREASON	= true

endtype (* TDISREASONtype *)

2.3.3   Transport service objects

Between occurring as a request and as an indication, the information encapsulated in a primitive is in transit between the endpoints of a connection. Since a primitive in the sense of [ISO 8072, 1984] is something which occurs *at* an endpoint, it is reasonable that another representation should be used for the information while it is in transit *between* the endpoints. The notion of a transport service object, modelled here by sort *TSO*, is introduced to satisfy this need.

For each primitive there is an identifiable object corresponding to that primitive. This is modelled in the formal specification by providing an operation, *object*, which maps primitives to objects.

Now typically it will be necessary, given a request from a user, firstly to transform it into an object for transmission through the service, and secondly to transform that object into an indication for delivery to the other user. Where *object* models the first of these transformations (and incidentally also maps indications to objects), operation *indication* models the second transformation.

It is perhaps interesting to note that for every object a corresponding indication exists, but a corresponding request need not. In particular there is no request corresponding to a service provider initiated T-DISCONNECT object. So there would have been some problems in trying to define an operation to map objects to requests, since intuitively such an operation would not be total. Fortunately its definition is not necessary here.

It is necessary to be able to distinguish different kinds of object and, as for primitives, a number of testing operations are defined. *TSOtype* is an enrichment of *TSPtype* and so use may be made of the earlier definitions of the tests on primitives to simplify the required equations.

type TSOtype
is
      TSPtype
with
sorts
      TSO
opns
      object   : TSP -> TSO
      indication : TSO -> TSP

```
        isTCON,    isTCAK,
        isTDT,     isTDT,
        isTEX,
        isTDIS            : TSO -> BOOL
        isProviderTDIS  : TSO -> BOOL

        _ == _            : TSO, TSO -> BOOL
eqns
forall
        tsp               : TSP,
        tso, tso1, tso2   : TSO,
        ta, ta1, ta2      : TA,
        teo               : TEXOPTION,
        tq                : TQOS,
        td                : TDATA,
        tdr               : TDISREASON

ofsort  TSP
        indication (object (TCONreq (ta1, ta2, teo, tq, td)))
                        = TCONind (ta1, ta2, teo, tq, td);
        indication (object (TCONind (ta1, ta2, teo, tq, td)))
                        = TCONind (ta1, ta2, teo, tq, td);
        indication (object (TCONresp (ta, teo, tq, td)))
                        = TCONconf (ta, teo, tq, td);
        indication (object (TCONconf (ta, teo, tq, td)))
                        = TCONconf (ta, teo, tq, td);
        indication (object (TDTreq (td)))    = TDTind (td);
        indication (object (TDTind (td)))    = TDTind (td);
        indication (object (TEXreq (td)))    = TEXind (td);
        indication (object (TEXind (td)))    = TEXind (td);
        indication (object (TDISreq (td)))
                        = TDISind (userTDISREASON, td);
        indication (object (TDISind (tdr, td)))
                        = TDISind (tdr, td);

ofsort  BOOL
        isTCON (object (tsp))    = isTCON (tsp);
        isTCAK (object (tsp))    = isTCAK (tsp);
        isTDT (object (tsp))     = isTDT (tsp);
        isTEX (object (tsp))     = isTEX (tsp);
        isTDIS (object (tsp))    = isTDIS (tsp);

        isTDISind (tsp) = false
              = >    isProviderTDIS (object (tsp))        = false;
        isProviderTDIS
              (object (TDISind (userTDREASON, td)))       = false;
        isProviderTDIS
              (object(TDISind (providerTDISREASON, td)))  = true;
```

$$tso1 = = tso2 = indication(tso1) = = indication(tso2)$$

endtype (* TSOtype *)

2.3.4 Transport service media

While in transit between endpoints, objects may be modelled as being in a medium provided by the service. The nature of this abstract medium is quite complex, involving not only simple transmission of objects, but also possible changes to the information contained in certain objects, together with possible addition, reordering and destruction of objects.

The specification of the medium is given in five stages:

(a) specification of a basic first-in-first-out (FIFO) medium,
(b) specification of the possible changes to information contained in objects,
(c) specification of the valid additions of objects to the medium,
(d) specification of the valid reorderings and destructions of objects, and
(e) specification of the combined effect of the above changes to objects in the medium.

2.3.4.1 Basic transport service media

The basic medium is simply a FIFO queue. Two operations are provided to construct media: a constant, *empty*, denoting the empty medium; and an operation, $+ - -$, to append an object to an existing medium. For example if *tso*1 and *tso*2 denote objects, then $(tso2 + - - (tso1 + - - empty))$ denotes a medium with precisely two elements, with *tso*1 at its head.

Given a medium, *m*, it is desirable to be able to ascertain which object, if any, is at its head, and what would remain if the head were removed. At first sight the solution is to define operations *head* and *tail* to give the leading object and remaining medium respectively. However a problem occurs in the case where the medium is empty. The intuitive notions behind *head* and *tail* constitute only partial functions on media: there is neither a head nor a tail of an empty medium. The solution adopted here is to replace the two proposed partial functions by a sort of 'inverse'. Instead of defining two operations to decompose the given medium into its component parts, an operation is defined which, given suitable values of a 'head' and a 'tail', will re-compose the medium from which they could have been extracted. The operation $- - +$ does precisely this. Since every re-composed medium must have at least one element (its head), that medium is equivalent to some other medium in which the head object was the first object appended, and this is reflected in the two equations relating $+ - -$ to $- - +$.

Lastly, the apparently inevitable Boolean equality operation is defined over media.

type BASICMEDIUMtype
is
        TSOtype
with
sorts
        MEDIUM
opns
        empty   : - > MEDIUM
        _ + - -_   : TSO, MEDIUM - > MEDIUM
        _ - - +_   : MEDIUM, TSO - > MEDIUM
        _ = =_   : MEDIUM, MEDIUM - > BOOL
eqns
forall
        m   : MEDIUM,
        tso, tso1, tso2   : TSO,
ofsort TSO
        tso + - - empty   = empty - - + tso;
        (tso2 + - - (m - - + tso1))   = ((tso2 + - - m) - - + tso1);

        empty = = empty   = true;
        (tso2 + - - m2) = = empty   = false;
        empty = = (tso1 + - - m1)   = false;
        (tso2 + - - m2) = = (tso1 + - - m1)
            = (tso2 = = tso1) and (m2 = = m1)

endtype (* BASICMEDIUMtype *)

2.3.4.2   Provider degradation of the service requested
The data type definition, *DEGRADEDMEDIUM*, contains the information
relating to the service provider's ability to reduce the expedited option
selection and quality of service requested by the calling user in a T-
CONNECT request, prior to passing it to the called user as a T-CONNECT
indication.

The operation *isadegradationof* is overloaded in this definition to apply
both to single objects and also to media. An object, *tso* 2, is considered to be a
possible degradation of another object, *tso* 1, precisely when *tso* 1 is a
T-CONNECT object (but not a 'T-CONNECT-ACKNOWLEDGE' object)
and *tso* 2 can be derived from it by reducing or leaving unchanged the
expedited data option and quality of service parameters and leaving all other
components unchanged. Operation *isadegradationof*, defined over media,
gives *true* precisely when each element of its first argument medium is a
possible degradation of the corresponding object in the second argument
medium.

        type DEGRADEDMEDIUMtype
        is
                BASICMEDIUMtype

with
opns

isadegradationof	: TSO, TSO - > BOOL
isadegradationof	: MEDIUM, MEDIUM - > BOOL

eqns
forall

calling1, calling2,	
called1, called2	: TA,
teo1, teo2	: TEXOPTION,
tq1, tq2	: TQOS,
td1, td2	: TDATA,
tso1, tso2	: TSO,
m1, m2	: MEDIUM

ofsort BOOL

TCON(calling2, called2, teo2, tq2, td2) isadegradationof
   TCON(calling1, called1, teo1, tq1, td1)
       = ((calling2 = = calling1)
      and (called2 = = called1)
      and (teo2 < = teo1)
      and (tq2 < = tq1)
      and (td2 = = td1)
      );
(isTCON(tso2) or isTCON(tso1)) = false
  = > tso2 isadegradationof tso1
      = tso2 = = tso1;

ofsort BOOL

empty isadegradationof empty	= true;
empty isadegradationof (tso1 + − − m)	= false;
(tso2 + − − m2) isadegradationof empty	= false;
(tso2 + − − m2) isadegradationof tso1 + − − m1)	

       = ((tso2 isadegradationof tso1)
       and (m2 isadegradationof m1)
       );
endtype (* DEGRADEDMEDIUMtype *)

2.3.4.3 Provider disconnection of media
Data type *DISCONNECTEDMEDIUM* contains the information relating
to the service provider's ability to initiate transmission of a provider
T-DISCONNECT at any time during the lifetime of a connection.

A medium, *tso* 2, is considered to be a possible disconnection of
another, *tso* 1, if and only if *tso* 2 is formed by the appending of zero or
more T-DISCONNECT objects to *tso* 1. The appended T-DISCON-
NECTs should, of course, cite the provider as the cause of the disconnection.

type DISCONNECTEDMEDIUMtype
is
        DEGRADEDMEDIUMtype
with
opns
        isadisconnectionof   :MEDIUM, MEDIUM -> BOOL
eqns
forall tso, tso1   : TSO,
        m, m1   : MEDIUM

ofsort BOOL
        empty isadisconnectionof empty   = true;
        empty isadisconnectionof (tso + − − m)   = false;

        (tso1 + − − m1) isadisconnectionof m
                = ((((tso1 + − − m1) = = m)
                  or ((isProviderTDIS (tso1))
                        and (m1 isadisconnectionof m)
));
endtype (* DISCONNECTEDMEDIUMtype *)

2.3.4.4 *Reorderings of media*
Data type *REORDEREDMEDIUMtype* embodies the details relating to the
service provider's ability to reorder the messages in transit.

If a T-CONNECT object is immediately followed by a T-DISCONNECT
object in a medium, then the T-DISCONNECT may 'negate' the T-
CONNECT by, as it were, destroying both the T-CONNECT and itself. This
is justified since were the T-CONNECT delivered as an indication, it would
be immediately followed by the T-DISCONNECT, indicating termination of
the connection. Mutual destruction within the service obviates unnecessary
work by the called user in attempting to deal with the connection request.
This is the only pair of objects which can so negate each other, and this is
expressed formally in the definition of operation *negates*.

A T-DISCONNECT which immediately follows an object other than a
T-CONNECT object may destroy that object in the medium, and this
relation is modelled in the operation *destroys*.

Lastly, it is possible for T-EXPEDITED-DATA objects to overtake
T-DATA objects. This relation is given in operation *overtakes*.

Now a medium, *tso* 2, may validly be derived by the service from another,
tso 1, if it can be derived by a single application of one of the three
possibilities described above: negation, destruction, or overtaking.
Operation < < models this relationship, the equations identifying the four
cases:

(a, b) The single application of a reordering cannot increase the number of
        objects in a medium.
(c) An empty medium may result only where the original medium contains
    two objects which can negate each other.

(d) In all other cases, a medium can be derived either by applying one of the three possible changes to the two elements at the tail end of the medium, or by applying one further up the medium.

Lastly, operation *isareorderingof* is defined to model which media can be derived from which other media by multiple (zero of more) changes. The four cases are:

(a) Application of no change constitutes a valid reordering.
(b). A medium derived by application of a single change is a valid reordering.
(c) If one medium is a valid reordering of another, which is in turn a valid reordering of a third, then the first is also a valid reordering of the third (by applying the appropriate changes in sequence).
(d) If one medium is a reordering of another and they are not equal, then the second cannot be a reordering of the first. That is, application of one or more actual changes is irreversible.

type REORDEREDMEDIUMtype
is

      DISCONNECTEDMEDIUMtype

with
opns

      negates,
      destroys,
      _overtakes   :TSO, TSO -> BOOL

      _<<_,
      isareorderingof   : MEDIUM, MEDIUM -> BOOL

eqns
forall

      m, ma, m0, m1, m2 : MEDIUM,
      tso, tso0, tso1, tsoa : TSO

ofsort BOOL

      tso1 negates tso0
              = isTDIS(tso1) and isTCON(tso0);
      tso1 destroys tso0
              = isTDIS(tso1) and (not(isTCON(tso0)));
      tso1 overtakes tso0
              = isTEX(tso1) and isTDT(tso0);

      m << empty   = false;
      m << (tso + − − empty)   = false;

      empty << (tso1 + − − (tso0 + − − m))
        = (tso1 negates tso0) and (m == empty);

     (tsoa + − − ma) << (tso1 + − − (tso0 + − − m))
        = (((tso1 negates tso0)
           and((tsoa + − − ma) == m))
)

```
or ( (tso1 destroys tso0)
    and((tsoa + − − ma) = = (tso1 + − − m))
    )
or ( (tso1 overtakes tso0)
    and((tsoa + − − ma) = = (tso0 + − − (tso1 + − − m)))
    )
or ( (tsoa = = tso1)
    and(ma < < (tso0 + − − m))
    ) );
```

m is	areorderingof m	= true;
(m1	< < m0)	= true
	= > (m1 isareorderingof m0)	= true;
((m2 isareorderingof m1)		
	and (m1 isareorderingof m0))	= true
	= > (m2 isareorderingof m0)	= true;
((m1 isareorderingof m0)		
	and not(m1 = = m0))	= true
	= > (m0 isareorderingof m1)	= false

endtype (* REORDEREDMEDIUMtype *)

2.3.4.5   Valid transformations of the media

Now at any time the service may transform the media in its connections by any or all of the means described above: degradation, disconnection and reordering. The cumulative effect of these changes is expressed as the application of the individual changes in sequence. The order of the sequential application is significant, however.

In particular, the addition of any provider T-DISCONNECTs should precede the reordering of objects. Since the presence or absence of the trailing T-DISCONNECTs affects which reorderings are possible, it is important to ensure that no valid transformations are omitted as would be the case if provider T-DISCONNECTs were appended *after* reordering had been effected. For then the possibilities of provider T-DISCONNECTs destroying other objects would be omitted.

The point at which degradation is applied is not critical since neither of the other operations adds T-CONNECTs to the medium, and the net effect of degradation is the same whether provider T-DISCONNECTs destroy T-CONNECTs 'before' or after they are degraded!

Operation *isavalidtransformation* relates four intermediate stages in the transformation of a medium by the service. Each successive pair of media is related by a single change. In practice the media of particular interest will be the first and last of the arguments: that is into which media, $m4$, can the service transform a given medium, $m1$, at any stage.

type MEDIUMtype
is

        REORDEREDMEDIUMtype

with
opns
    isavalidtransformation
     : MEDIUM, MEDIUM, MEDIUM, MEDIUM -> BOOL
eqns
forall
    m1, m2, m3, m4 : MEDIUM,
ofsort BOOL
    isavalidtransformation (m1, m2, m3, m4)
                  = ((m2 isadegradationof m1)
                     and(m3 isadisconnectionof m2)
                     and(m4 isareorderingof m3)
)

endtype (* MEDIUMtype *)

2.3.5 Connection endpoint identifiers

The following three data type definitions all relate to connection endpoint identifiers.

2.3.5.1 *Transport connection endpoint identifiers*
The set of all transport connection endpoint identifiers is defined in type *TCEItype*. The definition is analogous to that of addresses, and no further explanation is given here.

type TCEItype
is
    BOOLtype
with
sorts
    TCEI
opns
    someTCEI : -> TCEI
    anotherTCEI: TCEI -> TCEI

    _ == _   : TCEI, TCEI -> BOOL
eqns
forall
    tcei1, tcei2 : TCEI
ofsort BOOL
    someTCEI == someTCEI   = true;
    someTCEI == anotherTCEI(tcei2)   = false;
    anotherTCEI(tcei1) == someTCEI   = false;
    anotherTCEI(tcei1) == anotherTCEI(tcei2)
                         = tcei1 == tcei2;

endtype (* TCEItype *)

2.3.5.2   Address and connection endpoint identifier pairs
Any given endpoint may be uniquely identified by its address and the
endpoint identifier within that address. In order to manipulate such unique
references, type *ENDPOINTtype* is introduced. Operation *endpoint*, given an
address and endpoint identifier, constructs the pair which uniquely identifies
the endpoint. The only operation required is that of equality of pairs.

type ENDPOINTtype
is

        TAtype,
        TCEItype
sorts

        ENDPOINT
opns

        endpoint   : TA, TCEI- > ENDPOINT
        _ = = _   : ENDPOINT, ENDPOINT - > BOOL
eqns
formalopns

        ta1, ta2   : TA,
        tcei1, tcei2 : TCEI
ofsort BOOL

        endpoint(ta1, tcei1) = = endpoint(ta2, tcei2)
                                    = (ta1 = = ta2) and (tcei1 = = tcei2)

endtype (* ENDPOINTtype *)

2.3.5.3   Sets of address and connection endpoint identifier pairs
It will be necessary, lastly, to construct and manipulate sets of address and
endpoint identifier pairs. Type *SETofENDPOINTtype* defines a suitable sort
and the requisite operations to construct an empty set, *empty*, add a pair to
an existing set, + , and remove a pair from a set, − . Additionally set
membership, *isin*, and its negation, *notin*, are defined.

type SETofENDPOINTtype
is

        ENDPOINTtype
sorts

        SETofENDPOINT
opns

        empty   : - > SETofENDPOINT
        _ + _   : SETofENDPOINT, ENDPOINT
                                            - > SETofENDPOINT

        isin ,
        notin : ENDPOINT, SETofENDPOINT
                                        - > BOOLEAN

$$\text{\_-\_} \qquad : \text{SETofENDPOINT, ENDPOINT}$$
$$\text{-> SETofENDPOINT}$$

eqns
forall

$$\text{p1, p2} \qquad : \text{ENDPOINT,}$$
$$\text{s} \qquad\qquad : \text{SETofENDPOINT}$$

ofsort BOOLEAN

p1 isin empty = false;
p1 isin (s + p2) = (p1 isin s) or (p1 = = p2);

p1 notin s   = not (p1 isin s);

ofsort SETofENDPOINT

empty − p2   = empty;
p2 = = p1 = true
        = > (s + p1) − p2 = s − p2;
p2 = = p1 = false
        = > (s + p1) − p2 = (s − p2) + p1;

endtype (* SETofENDPOINTtype *)

2.4 BEHAVIOUR EXPRESSIONS IN THEORY

2.4.1 Events and transitions

The basic element of a LOTOS behaviour is the *event*. An event is considered, at a chosen level of abstraction, to represent the potential occurrence of a single, indivisible action. Let a be such an event, and let B, B' be behaviour expressions. Then a *transition* is an assertion of the form

$$B \xrightarrow{\alpha} B'$$

This is interpreted as meaning that the behaviour denoted by B may initially engage in the event α, and thereafter behave in a manner denoted by B'.

Now a behaviour may be characterised by the set of all its possible transitions. In the case of a behaviour denoted by B which is defined in terms of other sub-behaviours B', B'' it is desirable to be able to define its behaviour in terms of its sub-behaviours. In terms of transitions, this means deriving the transitions of B from those of B' and B''.

A behaviour then may be defined by a set of axioms (in the form of transitions) and a set of derivation rules. An action is possible for a behaviour if and only if its occurrence can be derived from the axioms and derivation rules.

2.4.2 Inaction

The most primitive behaviour is known as *deadlock*. This behaviour is characterised by its inability to engage in any action. This is reflected in its

LOTOS representation, **stop**, which is characterised by the empty set of transitions: **stop** has neither axioms nor derivation rules.

2.4.3   Action prefix

Each event in LOTOS is structured as a finite sequence of values. In each case, the first of these values is of a special sort, known as a *gate*. Informally a gate may be thought of as representing a boundary, or communication channel, at or through which the other values may be communicated. Let g be a gate, and let $v_i(i: 1 \ldots n)$ be values other than gates. Then an event is a sequence

$$g . v_1. \cdots .v_n$$

In LOTOS each v_i may be denoted by a value expression, $E_i(i: 1 \ldots n)$, constructed from the operations defined in the abstract data types, and gate g may be denoted by a gate identifier, G. Then the behaviour denoted by the behaviour expression

$$G!E_1 \cdots !E_n; \ B$$

may initially engage only in the event $g . v_1. \cdots .v_n$ and thereafter behave like B. Formally, if v_i denotes the value of the expression $E_i(i: 1 \ldots n)$, and g the value of G,

$$(G!E_1 \cdots !E_n; \ B) \xrightarrow{g . v_1. \cdots .v_n} B$$

So for example, the behaviour

```
t!someTA!someTCEI!TCONreq( . . . )
;        t!someTA!someTCEI!TDISind(providerTDISREASON, . . . )
     ;        stop
```

initially allows communication of address *someTA*, endpoint identifier *someTCEI*, and some particular T-CONNECT request, *TCONreq*($\cdots$), and subsequently may accept the same address and endpoint identifier with a provider T-DISCONNECT indication, and thereafter it deadlocks.

2.4.4   Alternative behaviours

A behaviour which permits engagement in any one of a number of initial events may be constructed in LOTOS from a number of simpler behaviours, each of which offers a reduced set of initial events. For behaviours B_1, B_2 the behaviour $(B_1[]B_2)$("B_1 *or* B_2") may engage initially in any event which is possible either for B_1 or for B_2. The choice of which behaviour does occur is made on the first event, and may typically be chosen, or influenced, by the environment or user of $(B_1[]B_2)$.

If the initial event which does occur was possible only for B_1, then subsequent behaviour will be as determined by B_1; if initially possible only for B_2, then subsequent behaviour will be as determined by B_2. If, however, the event which occurs was possible for both B_1 and B_2, then the subsequent behaviour will be determined either by B_1 or by B_2, the choice being made nondeterministically: the environment, or user, may have no influence over the choice. Formally, [] satisfies the two derivation rules:

$$\frac{B_1 \xrightarrow{\alpha} B_1'}{(B_1[]B_2) \xrightarrow{\alpha} B_1'}$$

$$\frac{B_2 \xrightarrow{\alpha} B_2'}{(B_1[]B_2) \xrightarrow{\alpha} B_1'}$$

These are the only rules which [] satisfies.

Expanding the previous example, the following behaviour expression denotes the case where, after occurrence of the T-CONNECT request, either a provider T-DISCONNECT indication or a user T-DISCONNECT request may occur. In neither case are any further events possible.

```
t!someTA!someTCEI!TCONreq( ··· )
;      (          t!someTA!someTCEI!TDISind
                             (providerTDISREASON, . . . )
              ;      stop
       []          t!someTA!someTCEI!TDISreq
                             (userTDISREASON, . . . )
              ;      stop
       )
```

2.4.5 Nondeterminism

Another way of specifying nondeterminism, other than offering two identical events as alternatives, is to use an internal event, denoted by **i**. This is a special event which may occur entirely without the knowledge or participation of the user. So for example the behaviour $(\mathbf{i}; B_1)[](\mathbf{i}; B_2)$ may behave either like B_1 or like B_2. But since the choice between these behaviours is made on the first event, and in neither case has the user any influence on the first event, the user has no control over which of the behaviours B_1 and B_2 is ultimately offered. The user should therefore be prepared to accept either.

If only one alternative is prefixed by an **i**, as in $(G!E_1 \cdots !E_n; B_1)[](\mathbf{i}; B_2)$, then the user may or may not be offered the event on gate G, depending on whether the **i** occurs. What is certain is that the initial events of B_2 will always be possible.

2.4.6 Choice

Let B' be a behaviour expression, and S a sort name. Then the behaviour denoted by (**choice** x: $S[]B$) may engage initially in any event α, such that for some value expression E, of sort S, the behaviour denoted by $[E/x]B$ can engage in that event. That is, for each value, in the sort denoted by S, represented by an expression, E, (**choice** x: $S[]B$) is prepared to behave like $[E/x]B$. Formally, letting $[\![E]\!]$ be the value denoted by E, and $[\![S]\!]$ the sort denoted by S, (**choice** x: $S[]B$) satisfies the single derivation rule:

$$\frac{[\![E]\!] \in [\![S]\!], [E/x]B \xrightarrow{\alpha} B'}{(\textbf{choice } x\colon S[\,]B) \xrightarrow{\alpha} B'}$$

In general, a choice may be offered simultaneously over several sorts, by extending the notation, for $n \geq 2$, thus:

$$\begin{aligned}
&\textbf{choice } x_1\colon S_1, x_2\colon S_2, \cdots, x_n\colon S_n[\,]B \\
&\quad \triangleq \qquad \textbf{choice } x_1\colon S_1 \\
&\qquad\quad [] \qquad (\textbf{choice } x_2\colon S_2, \cdots, x_n\colon S_n[\,]B)
\end{aligned}$$

Similarly, further abbreviation is permitted for several variables of the same sort thus:

$$\begin{aligned}
&\textbf{choice } x_1, x_2, \ldots, x_n\colon S[\,]B \\
&\quad \triangleq \qquad \textbf{choice } x_1\colon S \\
&\qquad\quad [] \qquad (\textbf{choice } x_2, \cdots, x_n\colon S[\,]B)
\end{aligned}$$

2.4.7 Guarding

In LOTOS behaviours may be defined to be conditional in much the same way as equations in the data types. In the case of behaviour expressions such behaviours are known as *guarded behaviour expressions*, and are based on the guarded commands of [Dijkstra, 1975].

For value expressions E_1, E_2, and behaviour expression B, the behaviour expression $[E_1 = E_2] - > B$ ("*if $E_1 = E_2$ then B*") is interpreted as meaning that if the assertion $E_1 = E_2$ can be derived from the data type definitions in the enclosing context, then the behaviour described by B may occur. Otherwise, no actions may occur: that is, the behaviour is equivalent to **stop**. Formally this is expressed in the single derivation rule:

$$\frac{E_1 = E_2, B \xrightarrow{\alpha} B'}{([E_1 = E_2] - > B) \xrightarrow{\alpha} B'}$$

In combination with the general **choice** construct, this provides a powerful tool for specifying complex choices. For example, assume that m denotes some value of sort *MEDIUM*, and consider the following construction:

choice undelivered: MEDIUM, deliver: TSO
[]   [m = (undelivered − − + deliver)]
->   B

For each possible pair of values, *undelivered* and *deliver*, taken from *MEDIUM* and *TSO* respectively, a different possible behaviour is offered. If the medium denoted by *m* could be decomposed such that *deliver* was the foremost object on *m*, and *undelivered* constituted the rest of *m*, then the behaviour denoted by *B* would be offered. If, however, for a particular choice of *undelivered* and *deliver*, *m* could not be so decomposed, then no events would be offered. One particular case always excluded in this way is that where *m* is empty, since then there can be no valid decomposition into a 'head' and 'tail'.

The most common guards involve expressions of sort *BOOL*. In order to simplify many guards, the proposition $E = true$ may be abbreviated to E alone.

2.4.8 General action prefix

The combination of action prefix, **choice**, and guarding to govern events is such a common one that a compact notation is provided in LOTOS to capture the essence of these operators simultaneously. The behaviour

$G?s$: $S[E_1 = E_2]$; B

is defined to mean the same as

choice s: S
[] $[E_1 = E_2]$
-> $(G!s; B)$

This describes a behaviour which initially can engage in any event $g.v$ where v is the value of any expression E of the sort denoted by S, and where $[E/s]E_1 = [E/s]E_2$ can be derived.

As with the **choice** construct, a more general form is possible where multiple sorts are ranged over thus:

$g?s_1$: $S_1?s_2$: $S_2 \cdots ?s_n$: $S_n[E_1 = E_2]$; B
$\overset{\Delta}{=}$ **choice** s_1: S_1
         [] $(G!s_1?s_2$: $S_2 \cdots ?s_n$: $S_n[E_1 = E_2]$; $B)$

For example, consider the following behaviour expression:

t?ta:TA?tcei:TCEI?tsp2:TSP [isTDIS(tsp2)]
;   **stop**

This permits any event to occur at gate *t*, such that the values communicated are any address, any connection endpoint identifier, and any primitive respectively, subject to the qualification that the primitive communicated be a T-DISCONNECT (request or indication). Thereafter, no further events are possible.

2.4.9 Successful termination and sequencing

In order to distinguish successful termination from deadlock, a special behaviour, **exit**, is introduced. This behaviour does nothing but terminate successfully. Actual successful termination is represented by occurrence of an event at a distinguished gate, which is denoted here by δ. After terminating successfully **exit** can do nothing further: in effect it deadlocks. This is represented formally by the axiom:

$$\textbf{exit} \xrightarrow{\delta} \textbf{stop}$$

Behaviour **exit** is completely characterised by this transition.

Where a behaviour may terminate successfully it is reasonable to allow a subsequent behaviour to be enabled following that behaviour. For behaviours B_1 and B_2, $(B_1 >> B_2)$ ("B_1 *enables* B_2") may behave like B_1 up to the point where B_1 may terminate successfully. Thereafter behaviour may be determined by B_2. Since the compound behaviour does not itself terminate successfully where B_1 does, B_1's successful termination is hidden from the environment and is represented by an internal event in the resulting behaviour.

This is expressed formally in the two derivation rules which $B_1 >> B_2$ obeys. For $g \neq \delta$,

$$\frac{B_1 \xrightarrow{g.v_1.\cdots.v_n} B_1'}{B_1 >> B_2 \xrightarrow{g.v_1.\cdots.v_n} B_1' >> B_2}$$

and

$$\frac{B_1 \xrightarrow{\delta} B_1'}{B_1 >> B_2 \xrightarrow{i} B_2}$$

This construct also has a more general form which permits the communication of values from the first behaviour to the second.

The behaviour **exit**$(E_1, \cdots, E_n)$ communicates the value of $(E_1, \cdots, E_n)$ by engaging in the single event $\delta . [\![E_1]\!]. \cdots .[\![E_n]\!]$ thus:

$$\textbf{exit}(E_1, \cdots, E_n) \xrightarrow{\delta.[\![E_1]\!].\cdots.[\![E_n]\!]} \textbf{stop}$$

The corresponding enabling operation is denoted by $B_1 >> \textbf{accept } x_1: S_1, \cdots, x_n: S_n \textbf{ in } B_2$ and the corresponding behaviour is defined by the derivation rule, for $g \neq \delta$,

$$\frac{B_1 \xrightarrow{g.v_1.\cdots.v_n} B_1'}{B_1 >> \textbf{accept } x_1: S_1, \cdots, x_n: S_n \textbf{ in } B_2}$$
$$\xrightarrow{g.v_1.\cdots.v_n} B_1' >> \textbf{accept } x_1: S_1, \cdots, x_n: S_n \textbf{ in } B_2$$

together with the additional rule

$$\frac{B_1 \xrightarrow{\delta.[\![E_1]\!].\,\cdots\,.[\![E_n]\!]} B_1'}{\begin{array}{c}B_1 >> \textbf{accept } x_1: S_1, \,\cdots\, ,x_n: S_n \textbf{ in } B_2) \\ \xrightarrow{i} [E_1/x_1, \,\cdots\, ,E_n/x_n] B_2\end{array}}$$

for the case where B_1 terminates successfully.

2.4.10 Processes

A complete behaviour may be abstracted and named in a process definition of the form:

> **process**$p\ [K_1, \,\cdots\, ,K_n](x_1: S_1, \,\cdots\, ,x_m: S_m): f: =$
> $\quad B$
> **where**
> $\qquad \cdots$
> **endproc**

This defines p to denote a behaviour expression parameterised by a set of gates, $K_1, \,\cdots\, ,K_n$, and a set of value expressions $x_1, \,\cdots\, ,x_m$ of sorts $S_1, \,\cdots\, ,S_m$ respectively. The set of gate names must contain the names of all gates on which B may communicate.

The functionality of the process abstraction is denoted by f. This indicates whether or not the behaviour may terminate successfully, and if so, the sorts of the result values. The keyword **noexit** indicates that the behaviour, B, cannot terminate successfully. Where a process may terminate successfully, the functionality is denoted by **exit**$(S_1, \,\cdots\, ,S_k)$, where the $S_i(i: 1 \ldots k)$ are the sorts of the result values.

The **where** $\cdots$ clause is optional. If present it contains type and mutually recursive process definitions which are local to the behaviour expression B.

Within the scope of the definition of a process p, it may be instantiated by a reference of the form

$$p[G_1, \,\cdots\, ,G_n](E_1, \,\cdots\, ,E_m)$$

Let process p be as defined above, g_i be the value denoted by the $G_i(i: 1 \ldots n)$, and k_i be the value denoted by the K_i. Then for any instantiation of p a relabelling function, f, may be defined such that $f(k_i) \triangleq g_i$. The relabelling, $B_{[f]}$, of a behaviour expression, B, is defined for $k \neq \delta$ by:

$$\frac{B \xrightarrow{k.v_1.\,\cdots\,.v_k} B'}{B_{[f]} \xrightarrow{f(k).v_1.\,\cdots\,.v_k} B_{[f]}}$$

$$\frac{B \xrightarrow{\delta.v_1.\,\cdots\,.v_k} B'}{B_{[f]} \xrightarrow{\delta.v_1.\,\cdots\,.v_k} B_{[f]}}$$

Then the behaviour of an instantiation of p may be defined by

$$(p[G_1, \cdots, G_n](E_1, \cdots, E_m)) \triangleq ([E_1/x_1, \cdots, E_m/x_m]B)_{[/]}$$

2.4.11 Disabling

A repeated form of alternative is provided in the disabling operator, $[>$. The behaviour denoted by $(B_1[>B_2)$ ("B_1 *disabled by* B_2") behaves like B_1, but at every point prior to B_1's successful termination, the initial events of B_2 are also offered to the user. If an initial event from B_2 does occur then subsequent behaviour is determined exclusively by B_2. Behaviour $(B_1[>B_2)$ terminates successfully when either B_1 or B_2 does so.

Disabling satisfies the following derivation rules, for $g \neq \delta$:

$$\frac{B_1 \xrightarrow{g.v_1.\cdots.v_n} B_1'}{B_1[>B_2 \xrightarrow{g.v_1.\cdots.v_n} B_1'[>B_2}$$

$$\frac{B_2 \xrightarrow{g.v_1.\cdots.v_n} B_2'}{B_1[>B_2 \xrightarrow{g.v_1.\cdots.v_n} B_2'}$$

together with the following rule for successful termination of B_1:

$$\frac{B_1 \xrightarrow{\delta.v_1.\cdots.v_n} B_1'}{B_1[>B_2 \xrightarrow{\delta.v_1.\cdots.v_n} B_1'}$$

Note that in practice B_1' will always be **stop** in the last derivation rule as a consequence of the definition of a successful termination.

2.4.12 Concurrency

In the definition of distributed systems it is essential to have a means to describe concurrently executing components, in particular where those components do not interact directly. The LOTOS operator which allows expression of concurrency is the *interleaving* operator, $|||$. The behaviour $(B_1 ||| B_2)$ behaves like B_1 and B_2 acting independently simultaneously. Since the underlying semantic model allows only for single events to occur at any time, this is modelled by the interleaving of the events constituting the behaviours of B_1 and B_2 separately. The only exception to this is the events representing successful termination of B_1 and B_2. In that case, successful termination of the whole behaviour may occur only if and when it is possible for both component behaviours simultaneously: that is, successful termination must be *synchronised*. So $(B_1 \mid\mid\mid B_2)$ obeys the laws, for $g \neq \delta$,

$$\frac{B_1 \xrightarrow{g \,.\, v_1 \,.\, v_2 \,.\, \cdots \,.\, v_n} B_1'}{B_1 \mid\mid\mid B_2 \xrightarrow{g \,.\, v_1 \,.\, v_2 \,.\, \cdots \,.\, v_n} B_1' \mid\mid\mid B_2}$$

$$\frac{B_2 \xrightarrow{g \,.\, v_1 \,.\, v_2 \,.\, \cdots \,.\, v_n} B_2'}{B_1 \mid\mid\mid B_2 \xrightarrow{g \,.\, v_1 \,.\, v_2 \,.\, \cdots \,.\, v_n} B_1 \mid\mid\mid B_2'}$$

$$\frac{B_1 \xrightarrow{\delta \,.\, v_1 \,.\, v_2 \,.\, \cdots \,.\, v_n} B_1' \,,\, B_2 \xrightarrow{\delta \,.\, v_1 \,.\, v_2 \,.\, \cdots \,.\, v_n} B_2'}{B_1 \mid\mid\mid B_2 \xrightarrow{\delta \,.\, v_1 \,.\, v_2 \,.\, \cdots \,.\, v_n} \textbf{stop}}$$

2.4.13 Parallelism

The behaviour $(B_1 \mid\mid B_2)$ acts like B_1 and B_2 progressing in parallel. That is, $(B_1 \mid\mid B_2)$ can engage in an event if and only if B_1 and B_2 can engage in it simultaneously. Hence $(B_1 \mid\mid B_2)$ satisfies the single derivation rule:

$$\frac{B_1 \xrightarrow{\alpha} B_1' \,,\, B_2 \xrightarrow{\alpha} B_2'}{B_1 \mid\mid B_2 \xrightarrow{\alpha} B_1' \mid\mid B_2'}$$

It is this operation which forms the basis of the specification decomposition style employed in the following specification.

If B_1, B_2, are regarded as constraints, in the sense that an event may occur only if explicitly permitted by each process, then $(B_1 \mid\mid B_2)$ describes the behaviour which precisely satisfies both of the constraints embodied by B_1 and B_2 separately.

2.5 BEHAVIOUR EXPRESSIONS IN PRACTICE

2.5.1 Events

The events which are of interest in the specification are the occurrences of primitives. The nature of these primitives has been described earlier, but in describing a full transport service, the occurrence of each event must be distinguished not only by the value of the primitive but also by the (logical) location at which the primitive occurs. Now this location may be characterised by three values: the *service level* at which the event occurs (in this case Transport); the *service address* at which it occurs; and the *endpoint* within that address.

Since all events in the specification occur at a single, fixed service level this is simply modelled by the use of a single gate, *t*, at which all events occur. In the case of addresses and endpoint identifiers, multiple values are required and the data sorts *TA* and *TCEI* are employed.

If *ta*, *tcei* and *tsp* denote values of sorts *TA*, *TCEI* and *TSP* respectively, then all events will be of the form

   t.ta.tcei.tsp

2.5.2   The transport service

The specification of the service behaviour may be structured as a conjunction of constraints. In particular two kinds of constraint are identified: those which may be completely expressed in terms of a single connection (**process** *TConnections*) and those which mutually constrain multiple connections. In the case of the latter, two constraints are readily identified: service-wide resource control, dealing with the ability of the service to support particular aspects of service at any time (**process** *ResourceControl*); and allocation of unique address and endpoint identifier pairs to connection endpoints (**process** *TCIdentification*). This initial separation of concerns is expressed in the outermost level of the specification:

   specification TS [t]: **noexit**
           (* ... data types to be included here ... *)
   behaviour
           (TConnections [t]
           ‖   ResourceControl [t]
           ‖   TCIdentification [t]
)

   where
           (* ... definitions of TConnections, ResourceControl
                   and TCIdentification to be included here ... *)
   endspec

The use of the parallel operator, ‖, means that a particular behaviour may occur only if it is consistent with the requirements expressed in each of the three named component processes.

The constraints dealing with service-wide resource control and TCEI allocation are the simplest to express and are considered first.

2.5.3   Transport connection endpoint identification allocation

The following constraints are associated with the allocation of TCEIs:

(a) On establishing a connection endpoint (through occurrence of a T-CONNECT), a TCEI, unique within the address at which the connection is established, is associated with that endpoint.

(b) Occurrence of a primitive other than a T-CONNECT or a T-DISCON-NECT does not affect the set of address-TCEI pairs allocated.

(c) On releasing a connection endpoint (through occurrence of a T-DISCONNECT), the address-TCEI pair formerly associated with it is freed for possible re-use.

The process *TCIdentification* gives the LOTOS representation of these requirements.

The single parameter of process *TCIdentification*1 represents the set of address-TCEI pairs currently in use at any time. This set is initially empty, as indicated in the parameter to the instantiation of process *TCIdentification*1 in process *TCIdentification*.

The selection predicate qualifying the initial events of process *TCIdentification*1 precludes re-allocation of an address-TCEI pair currently in use, and subsequent behaviour is parameterised by the set of address-TCEI pairs in use after the initial event.

process TCIdentification [t]: **noexit**: =

    TCIdentification1 [t] (empty)

where

    process TCIdentification1 [t]
                  (inuse: SETofENDPOINT): **noexit**: =

        t?ta:TA?tcei:TCEI?tsp:TSP
          [isTCON(tsp)
          = = >(endpoint(ta, tcei) notin inuse)]
     ;   ([isTCON(tsp)]
              ->TCIdentification1 [t]
                        (inuse + endpoint(ta, tcei))
          [] [not (isTCON(tsp) or isTDIS(tsp))]
              ->TCIdentification1 [t] (inuse)
          [] [isTDIS(tsp)]
              ->TCIdentification1 [t]
                        (inuse − endpoint(ta, tcei))
)

    endproc (* TCIdentification1 *)

  endproc (*TCIdentification *)

2.5.4 Resource control

The following constraints are identified associated with service provider resource control:

(a) **A T-CONNECT request** may be refused at any endpoint at any time. This particular requirement is not explicitly a part of the TS definition [ISO 8072, 1984] but it is apparent that, in any finite system, such refusal to accept new connections is reasonable, if for no other reason than that resources within the service may become fully allocated to other connections.

(b) **A T-DATA request** may be refused at any endpoint at any time. This feature is known as *backpressure flow control* and may occur, for example, when no more buffer space is available within a connection to store further T-DATA requests.

(c) **A T-EXPEDITED-DATA request** may be refused at any endpoint at any time. This is another instance of backpressure flow control, but note that flow control on T-EXPEDITED-DATA primitives is independent of that on T-DATA primitives. Although it is stated in [ISO 8072, 1984] that T-EXPEDITED-DATA requests may *not* be refused because of prior acceptance of a T-DATA request, no indication is given as to when a T-EXPEDITED-DATA request *may* be refused. The assumption made here is that it is possible for the service, for some undefined reasons associated with resource management, to refuse T-EXPEDITED-DATA requests at any endpoint, at any time.

(d) **The service user** has no control over when T-CONNECT, T-DATA or T-EXPEDITED-DATA request primitives are refused.

Identifying the endpoints which may refuse primitives is equivalent to identifying those endpoints which may accept the primitives. In the LOTOS specification in **process** *ResourceControl* the endpoints at which the different primitives may be accepted are represented as sets of address-TCEI pairs. Any primitive may occur at any endpoint provided that it can be accepted there. The selection predicate effectively limits events to these latter cases.

The use of the leading **i** to prefix the visible events means that the choice of endpoints at which T-CONNECT, T-DATA and T-EXPEDITED-DATA request primitives are accepted is made non-deterministically, and hence without the knowledge of the user, as required.

```
process  ResourceControl [t]: noexit: =

        choice acceptTCONreq, acceptTDTreq,
               acceptTEXreq: SETofENDPOINT
    []      i
        ;       t?ta:TA?tcei:TCEI?tsp:TSP
                   [   (isTCONreq(tsp)
                              = = >(endpoint(ta, tcei)
                                      isin acceptTCONreq))
                   and(isTDTreq(tsp)
                              = = >(endpoint(ta, tcei)
                                      isin acceptTDTreq))
                   and(isTEXreq(tsp)
                              = = >(endpoint(ta, tcei)
                                      isin acceptTEXreq))
                   ]
                ;   ResourceControl [t]

    endproc (* ResourceControl *)
```

2.5.5 Individual transport connections

The service as a whole may support an unbounded number of individual connections within its lifetime. If **process** *TConnection* describes the constraints associated with any one individual connection, then the set of all potential connections which may be established during the lifetime of the service may be modelled by an interleaving of a potentially infinite number of individual connections thus:

> **process** TConnections [t]: **noexit**: =
>
> > (TConnection [t]
> > ||| TConnections [t]
> >)
>
> **where**
> > (* ... definition of TConnection ... *)
>
> **endproc** (*TConnections *)

The form of unguarded recursion is the only way in LOTOS to represent the interleaving of an unbounded number of processes. Note however that although this describes a potentially infinite number of concurrent connections, at any moment only a finite number of events may have occurred since the beginning of the service, and so only a finite number of connections may have been established.

2.5.6 A single transport connection

In the same way as it is possible to categorise the constraints on the service as a whole as pertaining either to single connections or to relations between those connections, so the constraints on a single connection may be separated into those which can be expressed in terms of events at a single endpoint, and those which relate events at opposite endpoints.

The constraints pertaining to endpoints (**process** *TCEPs*) may be partitioned into two independent parts: those dealing with the endpoint from which the connection was initiated (the calling endpoint); and those dealing with the endpoint accepting the connection (the called endpoint). In practice the behaviours of the two endpoints are similar and are represented here as two parameterised instances of a single process (**process** *TCEP*). The parameter type used to indicate the role (calling or called) played by an endpoint is defined locally within the definition of **process** *TConnection* and is simply a sort with two distinct values: *callingTCEPROLE* and *calledTCEPROLE*. The relative independence of the two endpoint constraints is indicated as the interleaving of the behaviours representing them.

A similar decomposition is adopted in the case of the constraints relating events at the opposite endpoints of a connection. In this case two independent behaviours are identified. These correspond to the flows of primitives in opposite directions: from the calling to the called endpoint, and vice versa.

The behaviours state the relations between occurrences of indications at one end and occurrences of requests at the other. It is found that these relations may be expressed in a uniform way without reference to the direction of flow.

The constraint on the whole connection, formalised in **process** *TConnection*, is simply the conjunction of the constraints imposed by the endpoints and by end-to-end primitive flow: on a given connection an event may occur only if it is possible both for an endpoint and as part of the valid flow of primitives between the endpoints of the connection.

> **process** TConnection [t]: **noexit**: =
>
> > TCEPs [t] ‖ TCEPAssociation
>
> **where**
> > **type** TCEPROLEtype
> > **is**
> > **sorts**
> > > TCEPROLE
> >
> > **opns**
> > > callingTCEPROLE,
> > > calledTCEPROLE   : -> TCEPROLE
> >
> > **eqns**
> > **endtype** (* TCEPROLEtype *)
> >
> > **process** TCEPs [t]: **noexit**: =
> > > TCEP [t] (callingTCEPROLE)
> > > ‖‖   TCEP [t] (calledTCEPROLE)
> >
> > **endproc** (* TCEPs *)
> >
> > **process** TCEPAssociation [t]: **noexit**: =
> > > TCEPAssoc [t] ‖‖‖ TCEPAssoc [t]
> >
> > **endproc** (* TCEPAssociation *)
> >
> > (* ... TCEP and TCEPAssoc ... *)
> > (* ... TCEPAddress and TCEPIdentification ... *)
>
> **endproc** (* TConnection *)

Note that two additional process definitions, *TCEPAddress* and *TCEP-Identification*, are defined within **process** *TConnection*. Although they are not instantiated in the behaviour expression of **process** *TConnection*, these processes are defined at this level since they are instantiated by both **process** *TCEP* and **process** *TCEPAssoc*, and so must be defined global to both of them.

2.5.7 A single transport connection endpoint

As noted above, the constraints associated with calling and called TCEPs are similar, and are specified by a single constraint. Three separate constraints may be identified which are expressible in terms of a single endpoint. These indicate the ways in which

(a) use of an address is controlled at an endpoint (**process** *TCEPAddress*),
(b) use of an endpoint identifier is controlled at an endpoint (**process** *TCEP-Identifier*), and
(c) the order of occurrence of primitives is controlled at an endpoint (**process** *TCEPPrimitiveOrdering*).

Only the last of these constraints depends on the role played by the endpoint in the connection.

> **process** TCEP [t] (role: TCEPROLE): **noexit**: =
>
> TCEPAddress [t]
> || TCEPIdentification [t]
> || TCEPPrimitiveOrdering [t] (role)
>
> **where**
> (* ... TCEPPrimitiveOrdering ... *)
>
> **endproc** (* endpoint *)

2.5.8 Address negotiation

The use of addresses by a connection endpoint is quite straightforward:

(a) On the first event at a connection endpoint, the address is negotiated with the user of the service.
(b) Once negotiated, the address used by the connection endpoint remains fixed for the duration of the connection.

This is modelled in LOTOS in an equally straightforward fashion. The **process** *TCEPAddress*1, given an address, permits any events to occur provided that they occur at the given address; and **process** *TCEPAddress* conducts the initial negotiation of address with the user, before proceeding to behave like *TCEPAddress* instantiated with the negotiated address.

> **process** TCEPAddress [t]: **noexit**: =
>
> t?ta:TA?tcei:TCEI?tsp:TSP
>
> ;   TCEIAddress1 [t] (ta)
>
> **where**
> **process** TCEPAddress1 [t] (ta: TA): **noexit**: =
>
> t!ta?tcei:TECI?tsp:TSP
> ;   TCEPAddress1 [t] (ta)
>
> **endproc** (* TCEPAddress1 *)
>
> **endproc** (* TCEPAddress *)

2.5.9   Endpoint identifier negotiation

The use of endpoint identifiers by a connection endpoint is similar to its use
of addresses:

(a) On the first event at a connection endpoint, the endpoint identifier is
    negotiated with the user of the service.
(b) Once negotiated, the endpoint identifier used by the connection endpoint
    remains fixed for the duration of the connection.

The LOTOS representation of these requirements is given in
process *TECPIdentification*.

> **process** TCEPIdentification [t]: **noexit**: =
>
>   t?ta:TA?tcei:TCEI?tsp:TSP
>   ;   TCEPIdentification1 [t] (tcei)
>
> **where**
>   **process** TCEPIdentification1 [t] (tcei: TCEI): **noexit**: =
>
>   t?ta:TA!tcei?tsp:TSP
>   ;   TCEPIdentification1 [t] (tcei)
>
>   **endproc** (* TCEPIdentification1 *)
>
> **endproc** (* TCEPIdentification *)

2.5.10   Primitive ordering

A number of phases may be identified through which an endpoint passes
during the lifetime of a connection.

(a) Initially an endpoint is in a connection phase, modelled here by process
    *ConnectionPhase*1. This phase encompasses only the occurrence of an
    initial T-CONNECT primitive at the endpoint.
(b) After occurrence of that initial primitive, during which expedited option
    and quality of service parameters are negotiated, the endpoint may enter
    the connection acknowledgement phase (process *ConnectionPhase*2)
    during which a 'T-CONNECT-ACKNOWLEDGE' may occur.
(c) Following completion of the connection acknowledge phase, data may
    be transferred. Whether or not T-EXPEDITED-DATA primitives may
    occur is dependent on the expedited option agreed during the connection
    acknowledgement phase.
(d) Finally, at any point after the connection phase has been completed, the
    disconnection phase may be entered, thereby disabling all other events at
    the endpoint.

The overall relation of the primitive ordering at an endpoint is stated
formally in process *TCEPPrimitiveOrdering*.

process TCEPPrimitiveOrdering [t]
          (role: TCEPROLE): **noexit**: =

          ConnectionPhase1 [t] (role)
     > >
     accept calling, called: TA, teo1: TEXOPTION, tq1: TQOS
     in   ((ConnectionPhase2 [t]
                              (role, calling, called, teo1, tq1)
               > >
               accept teo2:TEXOPTION, tq2:TQOS
               in   DataPhase [t] (teo2)
)
          [>   DisconnectionPhase [t]
)

where
          (* ... ConnectionPhase1, ConnectionPhase2,
               DataPhase, DisconnectionPhase ... *)

endproc (* TCEPPrimitiveOrdering *)

2.5.10.1 Connection Phase1

During the connection phase only a single event, communication of a
T-CONNECT primitive, may occur. Whether it is a request or indication
depends on the role being played by the endpoint. Quality of service and
expedited option parameters are negotiated during this phase and passed, on
successful termination, to the following behaviour, together with details of
the calling and called addresses.

process ConnectionPhase1 [t]
          (role: TCEPROLE):
               exit(TA, TA, TEXOPTION, TQOS): =

     choice calling, called: TA,
          teo: TEXOPTION, tq: TQOS, td: TDATA
     []   ([role = callingTCEPROLE]
          - >   t!calling?tcei:TCEI!TCONreq
                              (calling, called, teo, tq, td)
               ;   **exit** (calling, called, teo, tq)
          [] [role = calledTCEPROLE]
          - >   t!called?tcei:TCEI!TCONind
                              (calling, called, teo, tq, td)
               ;   **exit** (calling, called, teo, tq)
)

endproc (* ConnectionPhase1 *)

2.5.10.2   Connection Phase2

The primitive following the initial T-CONNECT request (indication) may be
a T-CONNECT confirm (response). However the response may not indicate

allowance of expedited data *unless* this was also negotiated in the preceding connection phase. Similarly the T-CONNECT response may not raise the quality of service previously requested in the indication.

```
process ConnectionPhase2 [t]
                (role: TCEPROLE), calling, called: TA,
                teo1: TEXOPTION, tq1: TQOS):
                exit(TEXOPTION): =

        choice responding: TA, teo2: TEXOPTION,
                tq2: TQOS, td: TDATA
        []      ([role = callingTCEPROLE]
        ->          t!calling?tcei:TCEI!TCONconf
                            (responding, teo2, tq2, td)
                ;   exit (teo2)
        [] [role = calledTCEPROLE]
        ->          t!called?tcei:TCEI!TCONresp
                            (called, teo2, tq2, td)
                            [(teo2 < = teo1) and (tq2 < = tq1)]
                ;   exit (teo2)
        )
        )

endproc (* ConnectionPhase2 *)
```

2.5.10.3 Data phase

In the data phase of a connection two kinds of primitives may occur: T-DATA and T-EXPEDITED-DATA. Occurrence of these is constrained as follows:

(a) A T-DATA primitive may always occur.
(b) A T-EXPEDITED-DATA primitive may occur only if supporting the expedited data option has previously been agreed for the connection in question.

```
process DataPhase [t] (teo: TEXOPTION): noexit: =

        (   t?ta:TA?tcei:TCEI?tsp:TSP [isTDT(tsp)]
            ;   DataPhase [t] (teo)
        []  [teo = acceptTEX]
        ->  t?ta:TA?tcei:TCEI?tsp:TSP [isTEX(tsp)]
            ;   DataPhase [t] (teo)
        )

endproc (* DataPhase *)
```

2.5.10.4 Disconnection phase

The disconnection phase is the simplest of the four phases. It begins, and ends, with the occurrence of a T-DISCONNECT. This marks the termination of a connection at one endpoint: no subsequent events are possible at that endpoint of the connection.

process DisconnectionPhase [t]: **noexit**: =

t?ta:TA?tcei:TCEI?tsp2:TSP [isTDIS(tsp2)]
;   **stop**

endproc (* DisconnectionPhase *)

2.5.11   Endpoint association

Events which occur at opposite endpoints of a connection are related by a complex association. This has already been simplified earlier by identifying that the flow of primitives in opposite directions on a connection may be treated independently. For such a uni-directional flow (**process** *TCEPAssoc*), the relation may be decomposed initially into a number of simpler relations thus:

(a) The relation between requests which have occurred and indications which may occur on a uni-directional flow should be maintained consistently (**process** *onewaytransfer*).
(b) All requests should occur at one end of the connection, whilst all indications should occur at the other. The constraints at opposite ends are independent of each other. Each constraint is further decomposed into three separate constraints, relating to uniformity of address (*TCEP-Address*), endpoint identification (*TCEPIdentification*), and whether requests (*TCEPReq*) or indications (*TCEPInd*) are permitted.

process TCEPAssoc [t]: **noexit**: =

onewaytransfer [t]
‖   ((TCEPAddress [t]
            ‖TCEPIdentification [t]
            ‖TCEPReq [t])
       ‖‖ (TCEPAddress [t]
            ‖TCEPIdentification [t]
            ‖TCEPInd [t])
)

where

process TCEPReq [t]: **noexit**: =

t?ta:TA?tcei:TCEI?tsp:TSP [isTreq(tsp)]
;   TCEPReq [t]

endproc(* TCEPReq *)

process TCEPInd [t]: **noexit**: =

t?ta:TA?teci:TECI?tsp:TSP [isTind(tsp)]
;   **TCEPInd** [t]

    endproc (* TCEPInd *)

    (* ... onewaytransfer ... *)

  endproc (* TCEPAssoc *)

2.5.12   Uni-directional primitive transfer

The uni-directional transfer of primitives may occur subject to the following constraints:

(a) Initially there are no undelivered primitives in the medium. This is represented in the initial parameter, *empty*, to **process** *onewaytransfer*1.
(b) Initially, a request may be accepted (*AcceptRequest*), or an undelivered indication delivered (*DeliverIndication*).
(c) After either a request has been accepted or an indication delivered, the state of the medium may be transformed by the service without the knowledge or influence of any user. Afterwards, the connection reverts to the state described in (b) above. This is formalised in **process** *Transform* which, it will be seen later, recursively instantiates **process** *onewaytransfer*1.

  process onewaytransfer [t]: **noexit**: =

     onewaytransfer1 [t] (empty)

where
    process onewaytransfer1 [t] (m: MEDIUM): **noexit**: =

      (AcceptRequest [t] (m)
      [] DeliverIndication [t] (m)
)   > >
      accept m1: MEDIUM
      in   Transform [t] (m1)

    endproc (* onewaytransfer1 *)

    (* ... AcceptRequest, DeliverIndication
        and Transform ... *)

  endproc (* onewaytransfer *)

2.5.12.1 *Acceptance of requests and confirmations*
The constraint associated with the acceptance of a request or response primitive is as follows:

(a) A primitive may occur, provided that it is a request (or response).
(b) Following acceptance of a primitive, the corresponding object is sent over the medium associated with the connection.

This is modelled in LOTOS by:

process AcceptRequest [t] (m: MEDIUM): **exit**(MEDIUM): =

t?ta:TA?tcei:TCEI?tsp:TSP [isTreq(tsp)]
;   **exit** ((object(tsp)) + − − m)

endproc (* AcceptRequest *)

2.5.12.2   Delivery of indications and confirmations
The constraints on the delivery of TSPs to a receiving user are:

(a) Whatever object, if any, is foremost in the medium may be delivered to the user in the form of the corresponding indication (or confirmation).
(b) Upon delivery to the user, the foremost object is removed from the medium.

process DeliverIndication [t] (m: MEDIUM): **exit**(MEDIUM): =

choice undelivered: MEDIUM, deliver: TSO
[]   [m = (undelivered − − + deliver)]
->   t?ta:TA?tcei:TCEI!indication(deliver)
;   **exit** (undelivered)

endproc (* DeliverIndication *)

2.5.12.3   Internal transformation of primitives
Between occurrence of requests and indications, the medium may be transformed by the provider as defined in type *REORDEREDMEDIUM-type*. However, which of the possible reorderings occurs in practice depends on the nature of the possible reorderings. Consider first the cases where the medium resulting after transformation is not empty.

(a) It is possible for the service to offer the initial object from any possible transformation of the medium.
(b) However, if it is possible for either a T-EXPEDITED-DATA or a T-DISCONNECT object to have progressed to the front of the medium (by respectively overtaking or destroying T-DATA objects), then the service may be unable, because of the irreversibility of those internal actions, to offer any primitives other than T-EXPEDITED-DATA or T-DISCONNECT to the user.
(c) Furthermore, if a T-DISCONNECT could have reached the front of the medium, it may also have irrecoverably destroyed preceding T-EXPEDITED-DATA objects. It is therefore possible that only T-DISCONNECT primitives may be offered.

These three cases correspond to the three nested successive alternatives in the **choice** expression in **process** *Transform*.
The last case to be considered is where the transformed medium is empty.

(d) An empty medium may occur either because the initial medium was itself empty, or because the initial object in the medium was a T-CONNECT. In the latter case it would be possible for a T-DISCONNECT (whether user or provider caused) to have destroyed all objects in the medium and lastly negated the leading T-CONNECT. Hence this case may arise as a result of irreversible internal action.

Following transformation of the medium, following behaviour is determined in each case by **process** *onewaytransfer*1.

process Transform [t] (m: MEDIUM): **noexit**: =

        choice m2, m3, m4: MEDIUM
        []   [isavalidtransformation (m1, m2, m3, m4)]
        ->   **(choice**   m5:MEDIUM, tso:TSO
        []   [m4 = (m5 − − + tso)]
        ->   (onewaytransfer1 [t] (m4)
              []   [isTEX(tso) or isTDIS(tso)]
              ->   i
                    ;   (onewaytransfer1 [t] (m4)
                       []   [isTDIS(tso)]
                       -> i
                         ; onewaytransfer1 [t] (m4)
)
)
        []   [m4 = empty]
        ->   i
           ;   onewaytransfer1 [t] (m4)
)
endproc (* Transform *)

2.6   CONCLUSION

The presentation of a relatively complete specification in LOTOS of a real distributed communications service has shown that the language is sufficiently expressive to address problems of this size. Furthermore it is noted that the features of the language permit the isolation of essentially independent features of the application and this helps greatly in controlling the complexity of individual parts of the specification, and in turn of the specification as a whole.

Two apparent deficiencies in the language arise from the data type definition sub-language. The first is the absence of an implicit Boolean equality operator which could be induced from the term equality operator, ' = '. This leads to long and tedious definition of Boolean equalities throughout the data types. The second is the absence of a convenient means to define non-total operators. This deficiency may be overcome by a little ingenuity, as in the case of the 're-constructor' operations, such as − − + to replace conventional *head* and *tail* selectors. However a facility to define explicit non-total operators would, it is proposed, have made certain parts of the specification simpler both to express and to understand.

Despite these minor deficiencies, LOTOS represents a major step forward in the application of formal specification languages to practical applications, not perhaps so much in its technical innovation, but rather in that it represents a recognition by a standardisation body of the need for, and benefits to be gained from, the use of formal methods in the development, and expression of industrial standards.

2.7 ACKNOWLEDGEMENTS

The following individuals and groups deserve particular thanks for their very useful comments, on earlier LOTOS specifications of the Transport Service, which have helped in writing this chapter: Ken Turner, Giuseppe Scollo, Juan Quemada, the ESPRIT/SEDOS Project, and the Advanced Networked Systems Architecture (ANSA) Project.

In addition, my thanks are due to the following groups which have assisted in the development of LOTOS and of earlier LOTOS specifications of the Transport Service from which the specification presented here has been developed: ISO/TC97/SC21/WG1/FDT C, ISO/TC97/SC6/WG4 and BSI/IST/21/1/3.

2.8 REFERENCES

Dijkstra, E. W. (1975), 'Guarded Commands, Nondeterminacy, and Formal Derivation of Programs', *Commun. ACM*, **18** (8) 453–7.

DIS 8807 (1987), *Information Systems Processing – Open Systems Interconnection – LOTOS, a Formal Description Technique Based on the Temporal Ordering of Observational Behaviour*, Geneva: International Standards Organisation.

Ehrig, H. and Mahr, B. (1985), *Fundamentals of Algebraic Specification 1*, Berlin: Springer-Verlag.

Hoare, C. A. R. (1985), *Communicating Sequential Processes*, London: Prentice-Hall International.

ISO (1984), *TC97/SC21/N1534 – Guidelines for the Application of FDTs to OSI*, Geneva: International Standards Organisation.

ISO 7498 (1984), *Description of Basic Reference Model for Open Systems Interconnection*, Geneva: International Standards Organisation.

ISO 8072 (1984), *Information Processing Systems – Open Systems Interconnection – Transport Service Definition*, Geneva: International Standards Organisation.

MacLane, S. and Birkhoff, G. (1979), *Algebra*, 2nd edn. Collier MacMillan International.

Milner, A. J. R. G. (1980), *A Calculus of Communicating Systems. (Lecture Notes in Computer Science* **92**) Berlin: Springer-Verlag.

Tocher, A. J. ed. (1986), *ESPRIT Project 410, Technical Report SEDOS/87.7 (OSI Transport Service: A Constraint-Oriented Specification in LOTOS.)*, Commission of the European Communities: Brussels.

Chapter 3
Developing a High Level Specification Formalism

LI Da-Hai and T. S. E. MAIBAUM

3.1 INTRODUCTION

The objective of this chapter is to demonstrate the application of formal methods to the specification and verification of computer network protocols.

3.1.1 Traditional approaches to the construction of correct protocol specification

All the work in protocol specification takes one of two types of approach in constructing protocol specifications. For the sake of convenience of discussion, they will be called the 'partial' approach and the 'total' approach respectively.

3.1.1.1 The 'partial' approach
The essence of this approach is based on the notion that a protocol is 'a set of rules that governs the interaction of peer entities (in that protocol layer)'. In the construction of a protocol specification, attention is *only* paid to the specifications of each individual protocol entity. The correctness of a protocol specification is judged by a set of criteria on some general properties, such as deadlock freeness, loop freeness, completeness, etc. [Bochmann and Sunshine, 1980).

3.1.1.2 The 'total' approach
This approach is based on the notion that a protocol is a distributed implementation of a communication service, on the service(s) provided by the next lower protocol layer [Bochmann and Sunshine, 1980]. The construction of a protocol specification involves firstly constructing the specification of the service that the protocol is to provide, and that of the service provided by the lower layer; then constructing the specification for each protocol entity individually. To verify the correctness of a protocol specification, one has to prove that the composition of the specifications of each protocol entity and the specification of the service of the lower layer satisfies the protocol service specification [Hailpern, 1981; Vogt, 1982].

3.1.1.3   Their general problems

There are some apparent difficulties, both in the construction and verification of protocol specifications, with the conventional methods.

In the construction of the specification for a non-trivial protocol, the choice of specification for each protocol entity seems to be *too* arbitrary. Although certain heuristics [Hailpern, 1981] and rules [Rudin, 1982] have been laid down as guidelines for the construction of protocol specifications, there does not seem to be an easy way to make a protocol specification even nearly satisfactory, with respect to completeness and consistency, during the construction process. Over-specification is also a common phenomenon. So verification is absolutely essential if one is going to have any faith in a protocol specification.

Unfortunately, the process of verification is also very painful. The absence of the specification of the service that a protocol provides in the 'partial' approach makes verification of the protocol specification almost meaningless. [Sunshine, 1979]. Although the 'total' approach does give service specifications in order to carry out meaningful verifications, the verifications become very complicated for non-trivial protocols, such as the 3-way handshake connection establishment protocol [Kurose, 1982]. Many intermediate theorems are needed during the course of a verification, but it is hard to postulate effective and intuitive theorems. Several cycles of verification and modification may be needed before one can expect to obtain a reasonable protocol specification. The complexity (sometimes confusion) of a verification tends to make the result very much less convincing.

3.1.1.4   Reasons for the difficulties

The problems associated with the 'partial' approach are simply due to a naive view of protocol systems. A protocol is a set of rules with which each protocol entity must comply both in response to users' requests and in interacting with its peer entities via the underlying layer.

The reason for the problems encountered by the 'total' approach, which are also shared by the 'partial' approach, lies in the way in which protocol specifications are constructed. It is essentially a single-step development from the protocol service specification.

This single-step method is quite effective in dealing with simple protocols (e.g. the Alternating Bit Protocol). But it becomes very deficient when the protocol becomes more complex. For a sophisticated protocol, each protocol entity deals with a large number of issues, which may be interrelated and involve coordination with its peer entities via the lower layer. So if one starts a protocol specification by focusing on each protocol entity, all the issues have to be dealt with immediately; but in practice, it is difficult to identify all the issues that are involved, and which contribute to the provision of the service, in this manner. So guessing the possible outcomes becomes the name of the game in constructing the specification for each protocol entity. This kind of approach can easily lead to over-specification, and incompleteness and inconsistency in a protocol specification become inherent.

Because the entity specifications are not always straightforwardly obtained from the protocol-service specification, it is inevitable that intermediate theorems are needed during the proof of the protocol specification. However, if the specification of each protocol entity is intangible, it is very hard to imagine how to construct effective as well as intuitive theorems on top of them. Furthermore, the possibility of incompleteness and inconsistency in a protocol specification means that one has to iterate the processes of verification and modification, in order to get a correct one.

We would like to clarify here that in the context of this chapter, by 'protocol verification' we mean the correctness of the specification of a protocol with respect to the specification of the service it provides ('design verification' [Sunshine, 1979]), rather than the correctness of the coding (program) of the protocol with respect to the specification of the protocol ('implementation verification' [Sunshine, 1979]).

3.1.1.5 What is a protocol in this context?

The ultimate purpose of a computer network is to provide to its remote users a communication service of one kind or another, by the coordination of its agents (computers, for example). A *protocol* is basically a set of agreed rules to which all the agents must adhere in order to provide such a service. To reduce their complexity, most computer network system designs are structured in a hierarchy of layers [Zimmerman, 1980] as depicted in Fig. 3.1.

The top layer provides a set of services to the ultimate users, while the bottom layer corresponds to the physical transmission medium.

Each layer is referred to as a *protocol layer*. A protocol layer is viewed as a black box by its users (i.e. the entities in the next higher layer) whose service

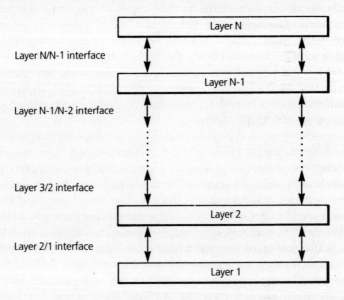

Fig. 3.1 Layered model of a computer network.

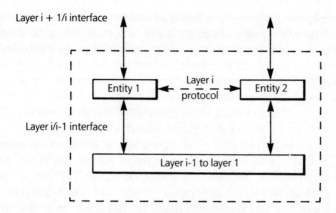

Fig. 3.2 Internal view of layer i.

can be accessed through a set of service primitive operations (like message sending and receiving operations) defined in its interface to the higher layer (cf. the concept of modules in program design [Parnas, 1977]).

To the implementor of a particular protocol layer (layer i, say) the view of the system is illustrated by Fig. 3.2. So a protocol at layer i can be more precisely defined as a *distributed implementation* of a required information transfer service by the set of the layer i peer entities, using the service provided by the next lower layer, $i - 1$.

3.1.1.6 Why is the formal specification of protocols important?

In order to build a large and complex computerised system, adequate specifications of the requirements and implementations are essential to ensure the quality of the system. People in the software engineering community have become increasingly aware of the inadequacy of natural languages (such as English) in specification, mainly due to their ambiguity. The alternative is to use *formal methods*, in which the syntax and the semantics of the specification language are precisely defined, and reasoning about a specification can be performed rigorously. The need for accurate but flexible specification in the design of protocols in distributed computer systems is obvious, as the systems are usually large in size and involve some quite sophisticated protocol algorithms to provide the necessary service to their users. Moreover, the specification of protocol problems faces some issues which are not usually of concern in the specification of a centralised computer system. Two of the major ones are:

(1) Each protocol has to be realised (programmed) on physically distributed entities (such as different computers on the network). This requires that the specification has to be unambiguous, so that the correct realisation of the protocol at each entity does provide the required service; and at the same time, the specification has to be flexible enough to allow different ways to realise the protocol specification at each entity, which can be heterogeneous in its characteristics.

(2) The physical transmission media available today are not very reliable, which can lead to the loss and corruption of data transmitted. So there is the need to specify whether the sending of data can lead to their delivery to the destination; this is generally referred to as the *liveness* property of data transmission. These observations motivate us to investigate the application of formal specification to protocols.

With the above background, the remainder of this chapter is organised as follows. Section 3.2 presents a general methodology, using a top-down step-wise refinement principle, for constructing protocol specifications. Section 3.3 discusses in detail the requirements on the formalism used for protocol specification. Section 3.4 concentrates on the definition of a particular formalism which is developed for protocol specification purposes, by giving its syntax and semantics, together with some properties that are useful in reasoning about given specifications. Section 3.5 demonstrates the application of the formalism, by specifying a token-passing protocol for a ring network. The concluding section, section 3.6, will discuss some interesting observations derived from this exercise.

3.2   TOP-DOWN STEP-WISE REFINEMENT OF PROTOCOL SPECIFICATIONS

This section briefly introduces a general methodology [Li, 1986], aimed at providing a systematic approach to the construction of *correct* protocol specifications.

3.2.1   The significance of service specifications

A communication protocol, in the context of the layered model of network architecture, is a distributed implementation of a required service, on the service(s) provided by the lower layer. The correctness of a protocol specification therefore means that the protocol specification and the specification of the service of the lower layer together imply the specification of the service that the protocol implements.

To illustrate this notion of protocol, an analogy to a simple example may be of some help. Let us consider the problem of mailing letters through post offices. If we treat post offices as *protocol entities*, then the *protocol-service* is the one that they provide to the general public, which is basically having the letters, sent by us, delivered to their destinations within some time limits according to the amount we pay. The transport services (*services of the lower layer*) available to the post offices are train delivery, air delivery and sea delivery; different methods of delivery have different speeds and costs. A certain set of rules (*protocol*) is observed by each post office in order to have letters delivered on time. It is obvious that such a mail service can only be accomplished with the coordination of the post offices all over the world, and with the assistance of various transportation services provided by other organisations; i.e. the role of the post offices is to *distributedly implement the mail service on top of the services available to them*. It is also apparent that the *correctness* of the rules complied with by each post office is ultimately judged by our observation of whether all (or most) of the mail is delivered undamaged and on time.

3.2.2   The top-down step-wise refinement principles

By identifying the scope for a protocol, we can have a clear notion of what the requirement on a protocol is, from the service that the protocol provides, and the sort of assumptions that the protocol can make, from the service(s) of the lower layer. A systematic approach can now be introduced to constructing a protocol specification from the specification of the required service, on top of the service(s) of the lower layer.

But before presenting the top-down step-wise refinement principles, the notion of *locality* in protocol specification needs to be explained.

3.2.2.1   *Locality of protocol-entity specifications*
The objective of any communication-protocol specification can be summarised by the following formula:

specification of the protocol's service
←   specification of the protocol + specification of the service(s) of the
       lower layer

where + is taken to be some kind of composition operator.

Because a protocol is a *distributed* implementation of its service on top of the service(s) of the lower layer, a protocol specification should consist of a set of specifications, each of which corresponds to a protocol entity; they are called *protocol-entity specifications*. Each protocol-entity specification must be *local*, in the sense that all the properties in a protocol-entity specification must be *realisable by the protocol entity itself, without* relying on the specifications of any of its peer entities or on the *global properties* of the underlying layer. The reason for this *locality* of entity specifications is simply that they should be at such a level of abstraction that the realisation of the protocol of each protocol entity is totally independent of those of the others.

Our post office example may help to illustrate the notion of *locality*. The overall protocol of a mailing system consists of sets of regulations (protocol-entity specifications), each of which is complied with by a post office. The regulations for each post office, such as the time for collection/delivery of mail to airports or railway stations, say, can all be carried out (or obeyed) by the post office concerned, without having to know what the regulations are for other post offices, or even the timetables of the transport organisations.

3.2.2.2   Top-down step-wise refinement

The difficulties in constructing and verifying protocol specifications, using the conventional methods, are mainly due to the complexity of the issues faced by each protocol entity, and the fact that the relations between a protocol-service specification and its protocol-entity specifications are not always straightforward [Li, 1986].

The problems with conventional methods for constructing protocol specifications are similar to those encountered by the bottom-up approach to program design. This observation motivates us to investigate a systematic approach for protocol specification, inspired by the well-known *top-down step-wise refinement* methodology [Wirth, 1971] applied to program design. The principles of the proposed methodology for constructing protocol specifications are:

(i)   Start the construction of the protocol specification from the specification of the protocol-service, rather than immediately focusing on the specification of each individual protocol entity;

(ii) Devise the protocol entity specifications from the protocol service specification in a *number* of *refinement* steps, rather than a single step;

(iii) Each refinement step is aimed at further 'localizing' the specification resulting from the previous step;

(iv) Each refinement step should be performed in such a way that the specification resulting from the previous step is still satisfied by the refinement of that specification;

(v)   Informally given protocol algorithms, such as the Alternating Bit Protocol or the token passing protocol, can be used as a guideline during the development;

(vi) The process of refinement is completed when the resultant specification can be partitioned into those corresponding to the protocol entity specifications (the local specifications) and those derivable from the service specification of the lower layer.

The intuition underlying the methodology is best illustrated by Fig. 3.3.

In summary, the methodology advocates a top-down step-wise refinement approach in constructing protocol specifications, by *gradually* decomposing the protocol service specification (global specification) into a set of protocol entity specifications (local specifications). This approach is in sharp contrast to conventional approaches, where the process of constructing a correct protocol specification is that of *synthesising* entity specifications into the protocol service specification (bottom-up!).

3.3   THE CHOICE OF A SPECIFICATION FORMALISM

This section briefly discusses the criteria for choosing a model for protocol specification, and gives the basic semantic concepts used in the specification of services as well as protocols.

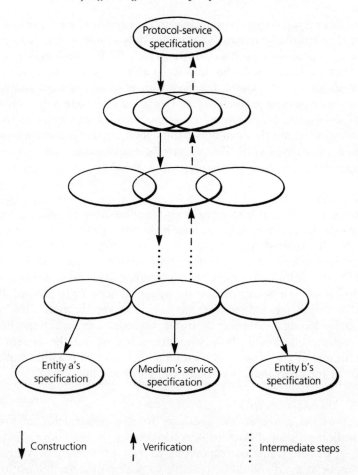

Fig. 3.3 Top-down step-wise refinement for the construction and the verification of protocol specification

3.3.1   Criteria for choosing a model

It is important to discuss the general criteria for choosing and developing an effective model as in the basis of protocol specification languages, because it is then possible to compare the one chosen with some of the existing ones with respect to these criteria.

3.3.1.1   Generality
The model should be *general* in two respects. One is that, besides its ability to capture the common features of *protocol algorithms*, it must also be capable of expressing those properties in *protocol services* which are of interest to the user. It has been observed that many existing works in protocol specification lack this ability in their models for expressing service properties [Bochmann and Sunshine, 1980].

The other respect is that the model should be capable of expressing different classes of protocol algorithms. That is, not only should it be able to express *data transfer* protocols, such as the Alternating Bit Protocol, and Stenning's Data Transfer Protocol, it should also be able to deal with *medium access control* protocols, such as the Ethernet Carrier-sense Protocol and various sorts of token passing protocol. Some models (e.g. the one in [Hailpern and Owicki, 1980]), can express data transfer protocols in a natural and straight-forward manner, but they can only handle medium access control protocols with great difficulty, if at all. The model to be described here has been success-fully applied to protocols of both types [Li, 1986].

3.3.1.2   Modularity
The model should be able to support *information hiding* at different levels of abstraction. This is absolutely essential in describing protocol systems with a hierarchically layered architecture. The most important feature of any specification (in general, not just the specification of protocol problems) is to present to the user *what* the object being specified does and *nothing more*; and the implementation details on *how* the system is actually to achieve its goal should be completely hidden from the user in its specification. This kind of information hiding is extremely desirable, because it can make a specification more comprehensible to those who are going to use the system being specified, and at the same time leaves a wide choice of possible implemen-tations for the programmers who are going to build the system.

3.3.1.3   Decomposability
To support the proposed methodology for the construction of protocol specifications, it should be possible to *decompose* the behaviour of a system into a set of behaviours corresponding to its component subsystems. And more importantly, it should be possible to perform the decomposition in a *step-wise* fashion. Some models, such as CCS [Milner CCS, 1980] and the Stream-processing Model [Kahn and MacQueen, 1977] are very effective in expressing the *composition* of subsystems into a global system; but they prohibit any intermediate development (decomposition) steps during the construction of protocol entity specifications from the protocol-service specification. In other words, these models *force* the specification of each protocol entity to be constructed individually, rather than allowing it to be developed in parallel from the protocol-service specification.

3.3.1.4   Simplicity and intuitivity
The model should be *simple*, in the sense that it should assume no more struc-tures than necessary to capture the essential concepts that are of interest to the user. The structures assumed by the model should be as simple as possible.

To be *intuitive*, a model should be able to reflect *directly* those matters of interest to the user, such as how the service of a communication system can be accessed, and the relationship between the messages sent and those that can be received by the users of the service. The ultimate purpose of a service specification is to enable the user to use the system being specified properly and effectively. A protocol specification is something that relates service specifications, so the user's view should still be evident in a protocol specification.

Simplicity and *intuitivity* can be of great help in the specification of systems in general, as they can ease the construction of specifications by closely mapping our understanding of the problems and the properties that can be expressed by the model; simple and intuitive models can also be a good basis for developing *comprehensible* specifications.

3.3.2 Basic semantic concepts

The basic semantic concepts involved in the specification of protocols are summarised as follows (see [Li, 1986] for more detailed discussion). They are: *operations* associated with communications; *message sequence (history)* that records data sent to (received from) a system with a particular service-primitive operation; *time* that relates the executions of service primitives; the notion of *event* corresponding to the availability of a message for collection; and the notions of *permission* and *obligation* to perform operations.

It is worthwhile to say a bit more about the specifications of operations. Firstly, it is natural to specify a service-primitive operation in a style similar to the declaration of a procedure header in a high-level programming language [Stenning, 1976; Hailpern, 1980]. For example, the *type* of a message transmission operation can be specified as:

> *Send*(*msg*: **User_Data_Unit; var** *status*: **Network_Status**)

However, the actual realisation of the operation does not have to be in the form (or using the mechanism) of a procedure in a high-level language; it can be a system interrupt, or even the direct manipulation of electric voltage. Secondly, the specification of the primitive for receiving a message, especially with an unreliable service, can take time-out as a parameter, e.g.:

> *Receive*(**var** *msg*: **User_Data_Unit**; *max_elapse_time*: **integer**;
>   **var** *status*: (time_out, ok, ..))

which is intended to mean that the operation will definitely terminate either due to the arrival of a message within the given time interval, or because no message has arrived when *max_elapse_time* expires after the operation is invoked; in the latter case, the value of *status* is expected to be time_out.

3.4 A LOGIC FORMALISM FOR SPECIFICATION OF PROTOCOLS

After identifying the basic semantic concepts for the specification of protocol problems in the previous section, the development of a logic formalism based on these concepts is now described and discussed. Section 3.4.1 gives an informal account of the language, while section 3.4.2 defines the language formally.

3.4.1   An informal introduction to the language

An informal account of various constructs of the logic formalism is given in this section. The aim is to present an intuitive understanding of the logic, and to relate the logic to protocol specification.

The most significant features of the language include:

- message sequence and message history
- action modal operators
- permission and obligation operators on actions
- temporal operators

The following subsections will describe each of them in detail, with respect to the formal representation, and give their intuitive interpretations in relation to service specification and protocol specification.

3.4.1.1   Message sequence and message history

The external behaviour of a protocol service or a protocol entity can be directly addressed by the sequences of messages sent to and received from it. Message sequences have frequently been used in reasoning about communication systems [Good and Cohen, 1978; Owicki, 1979; Hailpern and Owicki, 1980]. Some useful notations for describing message sequences are defined in the following paragraphs.

In the following definitions, the notations of *closed* and *open* intervals are assumed, i.e.

$$i \in [m, n] \quad \text{stands for} \quad m \leqslant i \leqslant n$$
$$i \in (m, n) \quad \text{stands for} \quad m < i < n$$
$$i \in [m, n) \quad \text{stands for} \quad m \leqslant i < n$$
$$i \in (m, n] \quad \text{stands for} \quad m < i \leqslant n$$

The length, or the number of messages, in a message sequence A is denoted by

$$|A|$$

If a message sequence A has elements (messages) u, v, w, x, it can be written as:

$$A = <u> <v> <w> <x>$$

If $|A| = n$, it can be written as:

$$A = <a_i>_{i=1}^{n}$$

where a_i denotes the i'th message in A.

The message sequence resulting from appending a message (m, say) to A is denoted by:

$A < m >$

The concatenation of two message sequences, A, B, say, is represented by:

$A . B$

Since the relationship between the orderings of messsages in different sequences is important in service and protocol specifications, there is a need to define *equality* and *initial subsequencing* relations on message sequences. Assuming A, B are message sequences respectively, the equality relation ' = ' is defined as:

$$A=B \equiv_{def} (A = <a_i>_{i=1}^k \wedge B = <b_j>_{j=1}^n \rightarrow n=k \wedge \forall i \in [1,n] . a_i=b_i)$$

In other words, two sequences are equal if they have identical messages, and the orderings of these messages are the same in both sequences.

The initial subsequence relation ' $\leqslant$ ' is defined as:

$$A \leqslant B \equiv_{def} (A = <a_i>_{i=1}^k \wedge B = <b_j>_{j=1}^n \rightarrow k \leqslant n \wedge \forall i \in [1,k] . a_i=b_i)$$

This simply says that A is an initial subsequence of B if it is identical to the first $|A|$ elements in B.

There is another curious but desirable initial subsequence relation, which we shall call the *loose initial-subsequence* relation or LIS for short. It is denoted by ' $\precsim$ '. The LIS relation is motivated by those communication services where not all messages can be received by the destination users, although the order of messages is preserved on delivery. The following example illustrates a simple case of the LIS relation, where $A \precsim B$:

$$A = <u><w><x><z>$$
$$B = <u><v><w><x><y><z>$$

Notice that elements v, y are missing from A compared with B, but the remaining messages in B are in the same order as those in A. Formally, the relation can be defined as:

$$A \precsim B$$
$$\equiv_{def} (A = <a_i>_{i=1}^k \wedge B = <b_j>_{j=1}^n$$
$$\rightarrow k \leqslant n$$
$$\wedge \forall i, j \in [1,k] (j > i \rightarrow$$
$$\exists i', j' \in [1,n] . (i' > i \wedge j' > i' \wedge a_i=b_{i'} \wedge a_j=b_{j'}))$$

Intuitively, the definition says that A is a LIS of B if for every pair of elements in A, there exists an identical pair in B, with the same ordering; e.g. if x, y are two elements in A with x coming before y, then there must be the same x, y occurring in B with x coming before y in B as well!

A *message history* is an unbounded message sequence that records the messages sent to (or received from) a system (a protocol layer or protocol entity) up to a point in time during a computation. The number of occurrences of a particular message (m, say), in a history variable X is denoted by:

    Count(X, m)

If the number of occurrences of a particular message, m, say, is unbounded in a message history X, it is stated as:

    $\mu c(X, m)$

This can be used to reflect the repeated transmission of a particular message over an unreliable transmission medium to overcome the possibility of loss of some instances of that message [Hailpern and Owicki, 1980].

3.4.1.2 Action modal operators

The idea here is to treat a service primitive as a *one-placed connective* on statements, thus forming a new statement from a given one. This notion originates from Pratt [Pratt, 1976], who considers a program as a one-placed connective on statements. To be more precise, if *OP* is some operation, and p is some statement, then a new statement can be formed, using Pratt's notation:

    $[OP]p$ (F1)

which is intended to mean 'after the action *OP* terminates, p will be true'.

Notice that the action modal operators introduced here are different from the classical logic connectives, in the sense that they do not have the truth functional preservation property which is possessed by the classical logic connectives. More specifically, a classical logic connective, such as the negation operator, is a truth function of the formula on which it operates; while the resultant statement formed by applying an action modal operator to a given statement is not a function of the given statement, as its truth value also depends on the action as well as the environment.

Example: In specifying the 'local behaviour' of a message transmission primitive *Send(m)*, in terms of its message history Y, say, assuming A is some message-sequence constant, one can say:

    $Y = A \rightarrow [Send(m)] \, Y = A < m >$

which directly reflects the local effect of the execution of the primitive, as having the message associated with the execution recorded on its message history.

It is interesting to compare Pratt's notation with that of Hoare:

    $p\{OP\}q$ (F2)

which syntactically associates an operation (program) with a two-placed connective on statements (p and q). It is definable in Pratt's notation as:

$p\rightarrow[OP]q$

And conversely, (F1) could be expressed in Hoare's notation as:

$true\{OP\}p$

where *true* is some universally true assertion (e.g. $-1 < 0$). There is work in protocol specification using Hoare's notation in defining service primitives, for example [Stenning, 1976; Hailpern and Owicki, 1980].

The theoretical significance of introducing Pratt's notation is that the study of *one-place connectives*, better known as *modal operators*, is a well-advanced topic in mathematical logic [Hughes and Cresswell, 1968; Thomason, 1970; Gabbay, 1976; Goldblatt, 1982]. The theoretical results from these works can be invaluable in the study of program specification.

The practical significance of using Pratt's notation is the ability to specify a protocol directly in terms of the service primitives that it is to provide and the service primitives that the protocol can make use of (i.e. those of the lower layer). For the existing protocol-specification formalisms, there is either the need to decode a service primitive into instantaneous events, see [Bochmann, 1978; Vogt, 1982] for example; or to state the roles of the service primitives *indirectly* via message histories [Hailpern and Owicki, 1980] in specifying protocol behaviour.

3.4.1.3 *Permission and obligation*
It is desirable to make statements about the permission to carry out a service primitive, and statements about the imposition of obligation in executing certain service primitives. Two operators on service primitives, **permit** and **obl**, are thus introduced to handle such requirements.

Assuming OP is a service primitive operation, the statement:

permit(OP)

should be read as 'OP is permitted to be performed'. The intended meaning of the statement formed by:

obl(OP)

is that 'the operation OP is obliged to be carried out'.

The notions of permission and obligation in specifying computing systems are due to Samit Khosla of Imperial College London, with his work on database specifications [Khosla, 1988]. N. Minsky also discusses a similar notion of permission in database systems [Minsky, 1985], but, unlike the former, no formal semantics are provided.

3.4.1.4 *Temporal operators*
Temporal relationships are also important in specifying protocol problems, especially liveness properties. Some temporal connectives on statements are used in the logic formalism developed here. Assuming that p is some statement, and t is an integer denoting time (which can be negative to represent the past), the following temporal operators are introduced.

The simplest temporal connective $\mathbf{O}(t)$ can form a new statement from a given statement p:

$\mathbf{O}(t)p$

which has the meaning of 'at t units of time from now, p will be (or was, if t is negative) true'.

In practice, it is not always interesting to state properties at an exact point in time; it is quite acceptable to talk about 'intervals' of time during which some properties are true. The connectives $[t]$ and $<t>$ are introduced in order to address properties that hold in a given interval of time. The statement given by:

$[t]p$

is intended to be read as 'p will be (or was, if t is negative) true *throughout* the period of t units of time from now'. The intuitive meaning of the statement

$<t>p$

is, on the other hand, 'p will be (or was) true at *some* point in time within the period of t units of time from now'. These explicitly quantified temporal connectives are especially useful in defining medium access control protocols, e.g. the token passing protocol, and the Ethernet Carrier Sense Multi Access Protocol, where the timing of actions can be critical.

If one is not terribly interested in the *exact* time interval in a specification, the connectives $\square$ and $\diamondsuit$ can be used to state those temporal properties with respect to the *entire* future interval of the computation from a given point in time. Intuitively,

$\square p$

is supposed to say that 'p will be true from now until the end of the computation'. And

$\diamondsuit p$

has the intuitive meaning of 'p will be true at some point in time that is between now and the end of the computation'.

If one is interested in the past tense, $\boxminus$ and $\diamondsuit$ are a pair of temporal connectives symmetrical to $\square$ and $\diamondsuit$.

$\boxminus p$

has the meaning of 'p has been true from the start of the computation until now'. And

$\diamondsuit p$

is interpreted as 'p was true at some point in time since the start of the computation'.

The use of *temporal connectives* in studying computations was initiated by Pnueli [Pnueli, 1977] and Kroger [Kroger, 1977]. Pnueli defines the temporal connectives □ and ◇, together with a couple of others in his temporal logic; while Kroger, in his *LAR – Logic of Algorithmic Reasoning*, introduces the notion of $O(t)$. ($O(t)$ is actually due to Shasha *et al.* [Shasha *et al.*, 1983]; Kroger uses the notation *square^t* in [Kroger, 1977]). Since then, much work has been carried out to use and extend temporal logic to study concurrent and distributed computing systems. [Lamport, 1980; Clark and Emerson, 1981; Nguyen *et al.*, 1985; Stark, 1984; Barringer *et al.*, 1984; Moszkowski, 1983] are some notable examples. Brent Hailpern is the first researcher to use temporal logic to specify protocols (the Alternating Bit Protocol and Stenning's Data Transfer Protocol) [Hailpern and Owicki, 1980]. Dennis Shasha *et al.* use a formalism based on Kroger's LAR to specify the Ethernet Carrier Sense Multi Access Protocol [Shasha *et al.*, 1983]. (The survey in [Li, 1986] gives a more detailed account of these works.)

3.4.2 Formal definition of the language

The logic system underlying the specification language is discussed in three parts, namely:

(1) *Syntax*, which defines the basic symbols of the logic, and the formation of expressions and formulae of the language;
(2) *Semantics*, which gives an interpretation of the language, for the purpose of protocol and service specifications;
(3) *Properties*, which are those semantic properties of the formalism useful for reasoning about complex formulae.

3.4.2.1 Syntax
The formulae of the language are built on three types of syntactic objects: expressions, operations (actions) and predicates.

Expressions   Expressions are built inductively as follows:

- Individual variables: X, Y, ...
- Functions: $f(e_1, e_2, ..., e_k)$, where $k \geq 0$, and $e_1, ..., e_k$ are expressions. The common arithmetic operations ' + ' ' − ', etc., are considered as functions, and constants are treated as functions without argument.

Operations (actions)   These are the ones corresponding to service primitives. Operations: $a(e_1, ..., e_k; u_1 ..., u_n)$, where $k, n \geq 0$, $e_1, ..., e_k$ are expressions, and $u_1, ..., u_n$ are the so called non-rigid designators, whose values can differ from state to state, like the variables in a programming language.

So the syntax of an operation is like that of a procedure in a high level programming language such as Pascal. A simple example of an operation is a message passing primitive to send messages:

   SEND(*msg, feed_back*)

where *msg* is the data to send out, and *feed_back* is only defined when the execution of the operation terminates; its value indicates whether the underlying system is in the proper working order to deliver the data.

Relating to high level programming language, the type of the example operation can be defined as:

SEND(*msg*: **User_Data_Unit**; **var** *feed_back*: **Status**)

Predicates   Predicates: $p(e_1, ..., e_k)$, where $k \geqslant 0$, $e_1, ..., e_k$ are expressions.

The class of closed formulae (i.e. formulae without free variables) comprises what are informally called 'assertions', or 'statements'. The formation rules for the formulae are as follows:

(1) Each predicate is a formula;
(2) If p, q are formulae, then so are $p \rightarrow q$, and $\neg p$;
(3) If x is a variable and p is a formula, then $\exists x.p$ and $\forall x.\text{p}$ are also formulae;
(4) If t is an integer expression, and p is a formula, then $\mathbf{O}(t)p$, $[t]p$, $<t>p$, $\Box p$, $\Diamond p$, $\boxminus p$, and $\diamondsuit p$ are also formulae;
(5) If c is an operation (action), then **permit**(c) and **obl**(c) are formulae;
(6) If c is an operation (action), and p is a formula, then $[c]p$, and p **during** c are formulae.

Using logical implication '$\rightarrow$' and negation '$\neg$', the other standard logical connectives are denoted by the following abbreviations:

● Disjunction: $(p \vee q)$ for $(\neg p \rightarrow q)$
● Conjunction: $(p \wedge q)$ for $(\neg p \rightarrow \neg q)$
● Equivalence: $(p \leftrightarrow q)$ for $(p \rightarrow q) \wedge (q \rightarrow p)$

3.4.2.2   Semantics

Having given the syntax of the language, the precise meanings of the notions introduced are to be defined formally here.

Model   A model of the language defined in section 3.4.1 is a structure:

$$M = (S, T, C, R, D, V)$$

where:
(1) S is a non-empty set, whose members are informally referred to as 'states';
(2) T is a natural number, giving the length of the computation in units of time. T could be infinite, but it always has an upper bound in practice, as there is always a time limit on how long a system can be in operation; furthermore, the execution of the message passing actions (sending a message, or receiving a message) can be guaranteed to terminate, either normally or 'abnormally' by, for example, the use of a time-out mechanism. Thus non-termination of the execution of an action has no significance in protocol specifications;
(3) R is an operator that associates with each operation (action), a, say, a binary relation R_a in S. That is, $R_a \subseteq S X S$;
(4) C denotes the computation. It is essentially a sequence of states indexed by time, $C = s_0 \, s_1 \, ... \, s_r$, where $s_i \in S$; so adjacent states in a computation

do not have to be distinct members of S, which reflects the situation where the system is in a particular state for more than one unit of time;

(5) D is a non-empty domain, containing integers and message sequences;

(6) V is a collection of mappings (indexed by time) that associates with each state s_t in C a *valuation*. For each variable X, V_t maps it to an element in D, that is

$$V_t(X) \in D$$

For each k-place function symbol, f, $V_t(f)$ is a function that maps a k-place tuple in D^k to a single element in D,

$$\forall t \in [0,T] . V_t(f) \in \{ D^k \rightarrow D \}$$

For each k-place predicate, p, $V_t(p)$ is interpreted similarly, but maps into *truth values*,

$$\forall t \in [0,T] . V_t(p) \in \{ false, true \}$$

For each action, a, $V_t(a)$ returns a value to indicate the status of the action at state s_t,

$$V_t(a) \in \{ during\_execution, not\_in\_execution \}$$

Notice that the semantics given here should keep the interpretations of function symbols and predicate symbols independent of time, because for our purposes they are *time-invariant*. Thus, the notations:

$$V(f) \quad and \quad V(p)$$

will be used as shorthand for:

$$\forall t \in [0,T] . V_t(f) \quad and \quad \forall t \in [0,T] . V_t(p)$$

respectively, where f is a function symbol and p is a predicate symbol.

Interpretation   Assume that $0 \leqslant t \leqslant T$ in the following interpretations.

(1) Expressions and Classical Formulae

v1) For each function $f(e_1, e_2, ..., e_k)$, where $k \geqslant 0$ and $e_1, e_2, ..., e_k$ are expressions,

$$V_t(f(e_1, e_2, ..., e_k)) = V(f)(V_t(e_1), V_t(e_2), ..., V_t(e_k))$$

i.e. the interpretation of a function at time t is the application of the function symbol to the values of its arguments at that time;

v2) For each predicate $p(e_1, e_2, ..., e_k)$, where $k \geqslant 0$ and $e_1, ..., e_k$ are expressions,

$$V_t(p(e_1, e_2, ..., e_k)) = V(p)(V_t(e_1), V_t(e_2), ..., V_t(e_k))$$

This is similar to the interpretation of function;

v3) $V_t(\neg w) = true$ iff $V_t(w) = false$;

v4) $V_t(p \rightarrow q) = true$ iff $V_t(p) = false$ or $V_t(q) = true$;

v5) $V_t(\exists x.w) = true$ iff for some b in the range of x, $V_t(w(x\backslash b)) = true$, where $w(x\backslash b)$ is the formula obtained by replacing each free occurrence of x in w by b;

v6) $V_t(\forall x.w) = true$ iff for all b in the range of x, $V_t(w(x\backslash b)) = true$, where $w(x\backslash b)$ has the same meaning as the one in v5;

For the abbreviations introduced in section 3.4.1, the following conditions hold:

$$V_t(p \wedge q) = true \quad \text{iff} \quad V_t(p) = true \text{ and } V_t(q) = true$$

$$V_t(p \vee q) = true \quad \text{iff} \quad V_t(p) = true \text{ or } V_t(q) = true$$

$$V_t(p \longleftrightarrow q) = true \quad \text{iff} \quad (V_t(p) = true \text{ if and only if } V_t(q) = true)$$

(2) Operations (actions)
Assume that a denotes some action in the following interpretations.

v7) $V_t(\textbf{permit}(a)) = true$ iff there exists s' belonging to S, such that $s_t R_a s'$;

v8) $V_t(\textbf{obl}(a)) = true$ iff $V_t(a) = during\_execution$;

v9) $V_t([a]w) = true$ iff there exists $t'.t < t' \leq T$ such that $s_t R_a s_{t'}$ implies $V_{t'}(w) = true$;

v10) $V_t(w \textbf{ During } a) = true$ iff $V_t(a) = during\_execution$ and there exists t', such that $t \leq t' \leq T$, $V_{t'}(a) = during\_execution$ and $V_{t'}(w) = true$; i.e. the formula holds if w becomes true at some point during the execution of a, which is going on now.

Note. It is assumed that the time intervals of different executions of the same action are disjoint and have no common boundary. This assumption is easily justified on the ground that we are not interested in the concurrent execution of the same action; furthermore, we can make the unit of time sufficiently small so that successive executions of the same action have no common time boundary to share.

v11) $V_t(\textbf{O}(t')w) = true$ iff $0 \leq t + t' \leq T$ and $V_{t+t'}(w) = true$;

v12) $V_t([t_0]w) = true$ iff $t_0 \geq 0$ implies for all t', such that $0 \leq t' \leq min(T, t_0 + t)$, $V_{t'}(w) = true$; and $t_0 < 0$ implies that for all t', such that $max(0, t + t_0) \leq t' \leq t$, $V_{t'}(w) = true$, where $min(m, n)$ is a function that returns the lesser of m and n, while $max(m, n)$ returns the larger one. Here, the value of time is limited to be within the bounds of the computation;

v13) $V_t(<t_0>w) = true$ iff $t_0 \geq 0$ implies there exists t', such that $0 \leq t' \leq min(T, t_0 + t)$, $V_{t'}(w) = true$; and $t_0 < 0$ implies that there exists t', such that $max(0, t + t_0) \leq t' \leq t$, $V_{t'}(w) = true$, where min, max are the same functions as they are in v12. Here the value of time is, again, limited within the bounds of the computation;

v14) $V_t(\square\ w) = true$ iff for all t', such that $t \leq t' \leq T$, $V_{t'}(w) = true$;

v15) $V_t(\Diamond\ w) = true$ iff there exists t', such that $t \leq t' \leq T$, $V_{t'}(w) = true$;

v16) $V_t(\boxminus\ w) = true$ iff for all t', such that $0 \leq t' \leq t$, $V_{t'}(w) = true$;

v17) $V_t(\diamondminus\ w) = true$ iff there exists t', such that $0 \leq t' \leq t$, $V_{t'}(w) = true$.

3.4.2.3 Some useful properties

Some important semantic properties of the language, which are sound with respect to the given valuations, are listed below, together with the axioms of the history variables. They become very useful in reasoning about the specifications given later in this chapter.

(1) Temporal properties In the following formulae, t, t_1, t_2 are integers which represent time.

p1) $O(t)\neg w \longleftrightarrow \neg O(t)w$;

p2) $O(0)w \longleftrightarrow w$;

p3) $O(t)(p \rightarrow q) \longleftrightarrow (O(t)p \rightarrow O(t)q)$;

p4) $O(t_1)O(t_2)w \longleftrightarrow O(t_1+t_2)w$;

p5) $[t]w \longleftrightarrow \neg <t>\neg w$;

p6) $O(t_1)<t_2>w \longleftrightarrow <t_2>O(t_1)w$;

p7) If t_1 and t_2 are of the same sign, i.e. both positive or both negative, then

$$<t_1><t_2>w \leftrightarrow <t>w$$

where $t = t_1 + t_2$. Fig. 3.4 clearly illustrates this property.

p8) On the other hand, if t_1 and t_2 are of opposite sign, the following condition holds:

$$<t_1><t_2>w \leftrightarrow <t_1>w \lor <t_2>w$$

The property becomes quite obvious with the help of Figure 3.5.

p9) $\diamondsuit$ and $\diamondsuit$ can be considered as special cases of $<t>$, so p5–p8 apply to them as well;

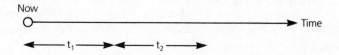

Fig. 3.4 Illustration of property p7.

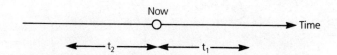

Fig. 3.5 Illustration of property p8.

p10) $[t]p \rightarrow \,<t>p$

p11) $[t]\forall x.p \longleftrightarrow \forall x.[t]p$

p12) $[t]\exists x.p \longleftrightarrow \exists x.[t]p$

p13) $<t>\forall x.p \longleftrightarrow \forall x.<t>p$

p14) $<t>\exists x.p \longleftrightarrow \exists x.<t>p$

p15) $[-t]O(t)p \rightarrow [t]p$

p16) $\diamondsuit\diamondsuit p \rightarrow \diamondsuit p$

p17) $\Box\,\Box p \rightarrow \Box p$

p18) $\diamondsuit\diamondsuit p \rightarrow \diamondsuit p$

p19) $\boxminus\,\boxminus p \rightarrow \boxminus p$

p20) $\diamondsuit(p \rightarrow q) \rightarrow (\diamondsuit p \rightarrow \diamondsuit q)$

A few interesting theorems can be deduced from these properties.

T1) $O(t_1)[t_2]w \longleftrightarrow [t_2]O(t_1)w$;

Proof:

$$
\begin{aligned}
&O(t_1)[t_2]w \\
&\longleftrightarrow O(t_1)\neg<t_2>\neg w && \text{by } p5) \\
&\longleftrightarrow \neg O(t_1)<t_2>\neg w && \text{by } p1) \\
&\longleftrightarrow \neg <t_2>O(t_1)\neg w && \text{by } p6) \\
&\longleftrightarrow \neg <t_2>\neg O(t_1)w && \text{by } p1) \\
&\longleftrightarrow [t_2]O(t_1)w && \text{by } p5)
\end{aligned}
$$

Q.E.D.

T2) If t_1, t_2 are of the same sign,

$$[t_1][t_2]w \leftrightarrow [t]w$$

where $t = t_1 + t_2$;

Proof:

$$
\begin{aligned}
&[t_1][t_2]w \\
&\longleftrightarrow \neg<t_1>\neg[t_2]w && \text{by } p5) \\
&\longleftrightarrow \neg<t_1>\neg(\neg<t_2>\neg w) && \text{by } p5) \\
&\longleftrightarrow \neg<t_1>\,<t_2>\neg w && \text{by } \neg\,\neg w = w \\
&\longleftrightarrow \neg<t_1+t_2>\neg w && \text{by } p7) \\
&\longleftrightarrow [t_1+t_2]w && \text{by } p5)
\end{aligned}
$$

Q.E.D.

T3) If t_1, t_2 are of opposite sign,

$[t_1][t_2]w \leftrightarrow [t_1]w \wedge [t_2]w$

Proof:

$$[t_1][t_2]w$$
$$\leftrightarrow \quad .... \quad same\ as\ in\ T2's\ proof\ until$$
$$\leftrightarrow \quad \neg <t_1> \ <t_2>\neg w$$
$$\leftrightarrow \quad \neg(\ <t_1>\neg w \ \vee \ <t_2>\neg w\ ) \qquad by\ p8)$$
$$\leftrightarrow \quad \neg <t_1>\neg w \ \wedge \ \neg <t_2>\neg w \qquad by\ \neg(\ p\ \vee\ q)\ \leftrightarrow\ \neg p\ \wedge\ \neg q$$
$$\leftrightarrow \quad [t_1]w \ \wedge \ [t_2]w \qquad\qquad\quad by\ p5)$$

Q.E.D.

(2) Axioms on the history variables   The notion of history variables for recording messages in and out of a module was introduced in section 3.3.2. There are a few axioms that define those properties of any given history variable that are true all the time.

HP1)   Let Q be some constant of message sequence, and X be any history variable,

$X = Q \rightarrow \square\ X \geqslant Q$

i.e. a history variable will never 'shrink' during an execution; and clearly the following condition also holds:

$X = Q \rightarrow \boxminus\ X \leqslant Q$

HP2)   If e is some message, and X a message history variable,

$e \in X \rightarrow \square\ e \in X$

that is, once a message has been recorded by a message-history variable, it will stay there for the rest of the computation; on the other hand, if it is not in a given message-history variable now, then it has never been recorded, which is expressed by the axiom:

$\neg(e \in X) \rightarrow \boxminus \neg(e \in X)$

HP3)   One other important property of any history variable is that it cannot record more than one message at the same time,

$X = Q<m> \rightarrow \diamondsuit\ X = Q$

(3) General Rule of Inference (Necessitation)   A tautology should hold during the entire computation from the start to the end, i.e. if P is a tautology, then $\square\ P$ and $\boxminus\ P$ both hold at any time of the given computation.

3.5   A TOKEN RING PROTOCOL

This section gives a flavour of the logic formalism introduced early on, by carrying out the specification of a token passing protocol on a ring network.

The key issue dealt with by the protocol is avoiding the collision of data during its transmission on the ring.

The section proceeds by, first, in section 3.5.1, presenting an informal account of the problem to be tackled, and then in section 3.5.2, building up the specification of the protocol using the given specification formalism, and following the top-down step-wise refinement methodology.

3.5.1 Informal description of the problem

Ring technology has gained great popularity in the design of local area networks (LAN). The Cambridge Ring [Needham, 1979], and the more recent IBM Token Ring for connecting IBM PCs and IBM-compatible microcomputers, are two of the most well-known ones.

Since the physical transmission line is shared among the stations connected to the ring, there is the possibility of data being corrupted during transmission due to data collisions. In order to provide a reliable data transmission service, various protocol algorithms have been proposed to avoid data collision occurring, by exerting *distributed* control on how the ring should be accessed. The most well-known ones are token-ring [Farber and Larson, 1972], slotted-ring [Pierce, 1972], and register-insertion-ring [Liu, 1978].

3.5.1.1 The scope of the protocol
In this environment each host computer interfaces with the physical ring via a microcomputer, called a **station**, as shown in Fig. 3.6.

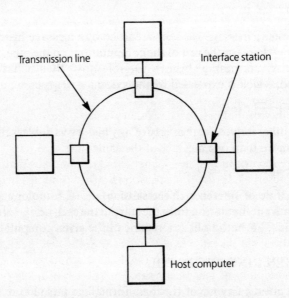

Fig. 3.6 Configuration of the ring network.

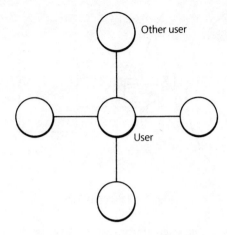

Fig. 3.7 A user's view of the system.

The interface is divided into three logical levels:

level 3: interfaces with the host, and provides a reliable message passing service;

level 2: provides a reliable end-to-end message passing service;

level 1: provides a broadcasting-type service using the underlying ring network.

The concern here is to implement the level 2 service on top of level 1, by using a token passing protocol, which avoids collision of messages during their transmission.

So the requirement is to provide a reliable transmission service between end-to-end users. That is, the user of the service at each station can send messages to a user at any other station. And a user is also equipped with a message receiving operation that can collect messages sent to it by any other station. Effectively, a given user views the system as being configured in a star topology, as shown in Fig. 3.7.

The reliability of the service means that the data sent will be delivered to the destination safely, and the order of messages is preserved during transmission.

The underlying medium is the ring network. It is obvious that the order of messages is preserved during transmission in a ring-topology network, as all the messages have to go through the same route. The communication is of broadcasting type, that is, each message sent can reach all the other stations on the network, and each message received by a station can be from any of the other stations on the ring. It is assumed that the medium itself removes the message after it has been circulating a full cycle in the ring, so there is neither the possibility of having the same message repeatedly received, nor the possibility of the user of the ring (i.e. a level 2 entity) receiving a message sent by itself. The ring is 'reliable' in the sense that the communication line

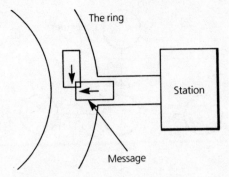

Fig. 3.8 Data collision.

will not break down, and each station will always be in working order. The only thing that can affect the safe delivery of data is data collision, which can happen when the event of a datum passing by a station coincides with the event of a datum output from that station, as illustrated in Fig. 3.8.

The following protocol is introduced to overcome the possibility of data collisions.

3.5.1.2 *The token passing protocol*
The token passing protocol used here is a very simple one. A (unique) control datum, called the *token*, is circulated from one station to another in the ring. Only the station possessing the token may transmit its messages, while the rest wait for their turns. This method is aimed at ensuring that only one station can transmit at a time, so the possibility of data collision can be eliminated.

To ensure that *every* station will have a chance to transmit, each station keeps an identical copy of a table containing the names of the stations on the ring; and at the end of its transmission, the station currently holding the token will pass the token on to the station whose name is next in the table.

3.5.2 The specification

The experiment is to be carried out using the methodology by giving the following specifications:

- service of level 2, user's view;
- service of level 1, protocol implementor's view;
- protocol, the rules that, using the level 1 service, provide the level 2 service.

3.5.2.1 *Level 2 service*
This is the user's view of the system. Let X_s, Y_s denote the sequences of the messages sent from and received by the user at station s (a level 3 entity) respectively, as shown in Fig. 3.9.

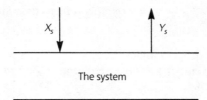

The system

Fig. 3.9 External view of the system by user at station s.

(1) Operations provided   Each station, s, is provided with the following operations to transmit and collect data.

$SEND_s(dest:$ **Station_Id;** $data:$ **User_Data_Unit)**
$$X=A \;\rightarrow\; [SEND_s\,(d\,,m\,)]X=A <(d\,,m\,)>$$

$RECEIVE_s(\text{var } source:$ **Station_Id;** $\text{var } data:$ **User_Data_Unit)**
$$Y=B \;\rightarrow\; [RECEIVE_s(d\,,m\,)] \;\exists\, s'\,,m'$$
$$(d=s'\wedge m=m'\wedge Y_s=B <(s'\,,m')>)$$

(2) The interface constraints   No user is allowed to send a message to itself from the network. This is asserted by

$$\text{(UI)} \qquad \neg\,\textbf{permit}(SEND_s(s, m))$$

(3) The global behaviour   Before presenting the specifications of the safety and liveness properties of the service, some definitions are necessary. In this chapter, a convention on the definitions of functions is adopted, i.e. a function is defined in the following Hope-like format [Burstall *et al.*, 1980]:

> syntax of the function   (function_name: domain→range)
> /* comments */
> — semantics of the function

In order to obtain just the user data from a message history variable, the function *User_data_only* is introduced, whose definition is:

$User\_data\_only:$ *sequence of* **(Station_Id, User_Data_Unit)**
$$\rightarrow \textit{sequence of } \textbf{User\_Data\_Unit}$$
$$— \; User\_data\_only(<s_i,\, m_i>_{i=1}^{n})=<m_i>_{i=1}^{n}$$

In the above definition, the first two lines give the syntax of the function, i.e. the type of the function, while the last line defines the meaning of the function.

To extract those data in a history variable that are sent to (or received from) a particular user, a projection function is introduced,

$Project:$ *sequence of* **(Station_Id, User_Data_Unit)**
X **Station_Id** $\rightarrow$ *sequence of* **(Station_Id, User_Data_Unit)**
$$— \; Project(<s_i,\, m_i>_{i=1}^{n},\, s) = <s,\, d_j>_{j=1}^{k}$$
$$\text{where } <s,\, d_j>_{j=1}^{k} \leq <s_i,\, m_i>_{i=1}^{n}$$
$$\text{and } \sum_{\forall m} Count(<s_i,\, m_i>_{i=1}^{n},\, <s,\, m>)=k$$

So $\sum_{\forall m} Count(\langle s_i, m_i \rangle \,_{i=1}^n, \langle s, m \rangle)$ simply returns the number of elements in the sequence

$\langle s_i, m_i \rangle \,_{i=1}^n$, with $s_i = s$ for $i = 1 \ldots n$.

To indicate the event of message arrival at a station, so that it can be collected, the predicate:

$AVAILABLE_s(d, m)$

is used, to signal that the message m, from station d, has just become available for retrieval at station s. This predicate is significant in relating an execution of the *SEND* operation to that of the *RECEIVE* operation at the peer site.

Safety   The safety property of the service is that messages are directed to the right destinations, with order being preserved on delivery. This is formally defined by:

(US) $User\_data\_only(Project(Y_d, s)) \leq$
$\qquad User\_data\_only(Project(X_s, d))$

Liveness   The service guarantees that every message sent will be delivered to the destination site, and if the receiving operation is invoked in time the message will be collected. These properties are formally stated as:

(UL1) $[SEND_s(d, m)] \diamondsuit AVAILABLE_d(s, m)$

i.e. every message sent will become available to be collected;

(UL2) $AVAILABLE_s(d, m)$ **During** $RECEIVE_s(s', m')$
$\qquad \rightarrow [RECEIVE_s(s', m')](s' = d \wedge m' = m)$

i.e. the availability of a message will lead to the termination of the *RECEIVE* operation with the incoming data.

3.5.2.2   Level 1 service
This is the system available to the implementor for providing the level 2 service. Assuming that α_s and β_s are the input and output history variables associated with station s on the network, the system can be illustrated by Fig. 3.10.

(1) The operations provided   Each station s is provided with both a data transmission operation and a data retrieval operation.

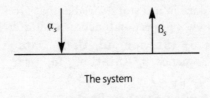

Fig. 3.10 External view of the ring at station s.

$PUT_s(m: \textbf{Packet})$
$\qquad \alpha_s = A \;\rightarrow\; [PUT_s(m)]\alpha_s = A <m>$
It is guaranteed to terminate.

$GET_s(\textbf{var } m: \textbf{Packet})$
$\qquad \beta_s = B \;\rightarrow\; [GET_s(m)] \; \exists \, m'(m = m' \;\wedge\; \beta_s = B <m'>)$

Here, **Packet** is the data type that is acceptable to the level 1 service.

(2) The interface constraints   There are no interface constraints imposed on the users of the service. That is, the order in which the service primitives are invoked is not important.

(3) The global behaviour   Again, as in the specification of the level 2 service, it is necessary to give some definitions first. Firstly, the predicate:

$ARRIVE_s(m)$

is associated with the event of message arrival to a station on the ring. When its value is true, it means that message m is at the station ready to be collected. The event of message arrival is assumed to be instantaneous.
The function:

$T(s_1, s_2)$

with s_1 and s_2 of type **Station_Id**, returns the time, as a positive integer, taken for a message to travel from station s_1 to station s_2. It can also be denoted by $T_{s1, s2}$.
The predicate:

$COLLISION(s)$

where s is again a station identifier, is associated with the event of data collision in the network. It can be defined more formally by:

Definition

(D0.1) $COLLISION(s) \equiv \exists \, m \, . \, ARRIVE_s(m) \textbf{ During } PUT_s$

That is, it is *true* if the event of message arrival at a particular station coincides with the execution of a message sending operation there.
To express the functionality of a broadcast-type communication service, where the messages received by a station can be from any of the other stations on the ring, it is desirable to define a function that, for a given set of message sequences, returns the set of all the possible sequences that can result from merging (interleaving) the given sequences. This function, denoted by $\cup$, is defined below, assuming that S_i, for $i \in [1, n]$, are sequences of messages.

Definition

(D0.2) $\displaystyle \bigcup_{i=1}^{n} S_i = \{ S \mid \forall \, i \in [1, n] \, . \, S_i \lesssim S \;\wedge\; |S| = \sum_{i=1}^{n} |S_i| \}$

Safety   One of the useful safety properties of the ring is that if there has not been any collision, then the messages received by a station must be from those sent by one of the others, and the messages are received in the same order as they are sent. This property is stated formally below:

$$(MS1) \quad \forall \, s \boxminus \neg COLLISION\,(s) \;\; \rightarrow \;\; \forall \, s' \, . \, \exists \, \pi \in \bigcup_{d \neq s'} \alpha_d \, . \, (\beta_{s'} \lesssim \pi)$$

That is, if data collision has not occurred so far, the sequence of messages received by a station must be a *loose initial-substance* (defined in section 3.4.1.1) of a sequence that results from an interleaving of all those sequences of messages sent by the other stations.

The property on the timing of message arrival is specified in the following axiom:

$$(MS2) \;\; ARRIVE_s\,(m)$$
$$\rightarrow \; \exists \, d \neq s \, . \, \exists \, m' \, . \, O(\text{-}T_{d,s})(true \; \textbf{During} \; PUT_s(m'))$$

Notice that in (MS2) if collision occurs then m' may not be equal to m. The latter may be corrupted data. So (MS2) effectively says that the medium will never generate extra data itself.

Liveness   The important liveness property of a ring, for implementing a reliable communication service, is that if no collision occurs in the future then every message sent by a station will be broadcast to the rest of the stations on the ring. This property is formally given by the following assertion:

$$(ML1) \qquad \forall \, s \Box \neg COLLISION\,(s)$$
$$\rightarrow \;\; \forall \, s' \, . \, [PUT_s(m)] \; \forall \, d \neq s' \, . \, O(T_{s',d})ARRIVE_d\,(m)$$

i.e. if no collision happens in the future, then every message sent will be successfully broadcast.

$$(ML2) \;\; ARRIVE_s\,(m') \; \textbf{During} \; GET_s(m) \;\; \rightarrow \;\; [GET_s(m)] \; m=m'$$

This one is similar to (UL2); it relates the executions of the *PUT* operations with the executions of the *GET* operations.

3.5.3   The protocol

Five refinement steps are involved in constructing the protocol specification, from the requirement specification for each individual protocol entity. The first step is concerned with the mapping of user data to protocol data, and the remaining steps are devoted to 'implementing' the data collision-free requirement.

Each step is to be presented along the following lines:

- a general description of the mechanism(s) introduced in the refinement;
- specification resulting from the refinement;
- identification of these axioms requiring further refinement;

- verification of the refinement against the specification resulting from the previous step.

3.5.3.1 Step 1

The objective of the step is to map the user data into protocol data on transmission, that is, to map the user data into a format that can be sent by the protocol entity to the underlying medium; and to map the protocol data back to user data on receiving them from the medium.

Since the medium provides a broadcast type communication service, data sent to the medium can then be received by *any* other station, and the data received can be from *any* other station. So some way to distinguish messages from (to) different stations is needed.

Here, we present the definition of the type of protocol data, and the definitions of some auxiliary functions to extract data associated with a particular station, as these will be valuable in the forthcoming specification.

(1) Definitions of protocol data type and auxiliary functions

Protocol data types   Two types of information will be sent to/received from the medium by a protocol entity. One carries user data, and the other carries control information. So **Packet**, the type of data acceptable to the medium, has two subtypes:

Packet = Protocol_Data_Unit + Protocol_Control_Unit

Protocol_Data_Unit is of the format:

data(*Source_id, Destination_id*: **Station_Id**; *msg:* **User_Data_Unit**)

Station_Id is the type of all the names of the stations on the ring. **Protocol_Control_Unit** will be explained later on when introducing token passing.

Functions   Firstly, some functions on protocol data are given as follows:

$Source\_id\_of$: **Protocol_Data_Unit** → **Station_Id**
/* Returns the source address of a data item */
—$Source\_id\_of$(data(s ,d ,m))=s

$Dest\_id\_of$: **Protocol_Data_Unit** → **Station_Id**
/* Returns the destination address of a data item */
—$Dest\_id\_of$(data(s ,d ,m))=d

Msg_of: **Protocol_Data_Unit** → **User_Data_Unit**
/* Returns the user message in the data item */
—Msg_of(data(s ,d ,m))=m

The following functions are on protocol data sequences:

Protocol_data_only: *Sequence of* **Packet**
$\rightarrow$ *Sequence of* **Protocol_Data_Unit**
/* Extracts the sequence of protocol data (discarding
protocol controls) from a given sequence of **Packets** */
——*Protocol_data_only*$(P)=P'$
Where $P' \lesssim P$
and $\forall d \in P$. d is **Protocol_Data_Unit** $\rightarrow d \in P'$
and $\forall d \in P'$. $Count(P',d)=Count(P,d)$

Recall that '$\lesssim$' is the loose initial-subsequence relation on sequences (see 3.4.1.1), so the order of elements (messages) is preserved by the above function.

Filter$_{source}$: *Sequence of* (**Protocol_Data_Unit** , **Station_Id**)
$\rightarrow$ *Sequence of* **Protocol_Data_Unit**
/* Returns the sequence of protocol data with the
given source address   */
——*Filter*$_{source}(P,s)=P'$
where $P' \lesssim P$
and $\forall m \in P'$. $Source\_id\_of(m)=s$
and $\forall m \in P'$. $Count(P',m)=Count(P,m)$

Filter$_{dest}$: *Sequence of* (**Protocol_Data_Unit** , **Station_Id**)
$\rightarrow$ *Sequence of* **Protocol_Data_Unit**
/* Returns the sequence of protocol data with the
given destination address   */
——*Filter*$_{dest}(P,d)=P'$
where $P' \lesssim P$
and $\forall m \in P'$. $Dest\_id\_of(m)=s$
and $\forall m \in P'$. $Count(P',m)=Count(P,m)$

Strip$_{source}$: *Sequence of* **Protocol_Data_Unit**
$\rightarrow$ *Sequence of* (**Station_Id**, **User_Data_Unit**)
/* Maps a sequence of protocol data to the corresponding
ones that are *sent* by a user   */
——*Strip*$_{source}(<S\_id_i,D\_id_i,m_i>_{i=1}^n)=<D\_id_i,m_i>_{i=1}^n$

Strip$_{dest}$: *Sequence of* **Protocol_Data_Unit**
$\rightarrow$ *Sequence of* (**Station_Id**, **User_Data_Unit**)
/* Maps a sequence of protocol data to the corresponding
ones that are *received* by a user   */
——*Strip*$_{dest}(<S\_id_i,D\_id_i,m_i>_{i=1}^n)=<S\_id_i,m_i>_{i=1}^n$

With these definitions, it is now possible to give the specification of the step.

(2) Refinement

Safety   All the data received by a user must be from those protocol data which are addressed to that user. The only safety axiom, (US), from the required service is replaced by the following ones:

(S1.1) $Y_d \leqslant Strip_{dest}(Filter_{dest}(Protocol\_data\_only(\beta_d),d))$

i.e. the data received by the user at station d must be from the protocol data addressed to d, which is received by the protocol entity there.

All the protocol data received from the medium with source address s and destination address d must originate from station s, with the order of messages being preserved during transmission; this property is stated by:

(S1.2) $Filter_{source}(Filter_{dest}(\beta_d,d),s) \leqslant Filter_{dest}(\alpha_s,d)$

All the protocol data sent by a protocol entity must be associated with its local user:

(S1.3) $Strip_{source}(Protocol\_data\_only(\alpha_s)) \leqslant X_s$

No station can issue protocol data whose source address is other than the address of the station at which the protocol entity resides:

(S1.4) $data(s\_id, d\_id, m) \in \alpha_s \rightarrow s\_id = s$

Liveness   The main concern here is that once a message has been sent by a user, it will be delivered to its destination eventually, so only (UL1) needs to be refined with the following axioms:

(L1.1) $[SEND_s(dest,m)] \diamondsuit obl(PUT_s(data(s,dest,m)))$

i.e. on getting a request from the user, the local protocol entity will act to send the corresponding protocol data to the medium.

(L1.2) $[PUT_s(p)] \diamondsuit ARRIVE_d(p)$
where $d = Dest\_id\_of(p)$

i.e. the protocol data sent will reach their destination.

(L1.3) $ARRIVE_d(p) \rightarrow obl(GET_d)$

i.e. no data arriving at a station will be ignored by the protocol entity there.

(L1.4) $ARRIVE_d(p')$ During $GET_d(p) \rightarrow [GET_d(p)]p = p'$

This axiom simply relates the event of message arrival with the execution of the *GET* operation.

(L1.5) $[GET_d(p)] (Dest\_id\_of(p) = d$
$\rightarrow \diamondsuit AVAILABLE_d(s\_id, m))$
where $s\_id = Source\_id\_of(p)$
and $m = Msg\_of(p)$

Axiom (L1.5) makes sure that if protocol data received are addressed to the owning station, then the user information will be made available for the user there to collect.

Lastly, (UL2), the other liveness axiom of the required service is retained as:

(L1.6) $\dot{AVAILABLE_d}(s',m')$ **During** $RECEIVE_d(s,m)$
$\rightarrow [RECEIVE_d(s, m)](m=m' \wedge s=s')$

(3) Further refinement needed

There is no need to refine any axioms from (S1.1) (S1.3) (S1.4) (L1.1) and (L1.3) – (L1.6), as they can be realised locally; each of them has history variables local only to the same protocol entity.

However, (S1.2) and (L1.2) can be supported by the underlying medium only if no data collision occurs (see the specification of the underlying medium). The rest of the refinement process will therefore concentrate on data-collision avoidance.

(4) Verification

The goal of verification is to show that

(US) $User\_data\_only(Project(Y_d,s))$
$\leq User\_data\_only(Project(X_s,d))$

and

(UL1) $[SEND_s(d,m)] \diamondsuit AVAILABLE_d(s,m)$

still hold.

Assuming that

$\alpha'_s=Protocol\_data\_only(\alpha_s)$
$\beta'_d=Protocol\_data\_only(\beta_d)$
$S_1=Filter_{dest}(\alpha'_s,d)$
$S_2=Filter_{source}(Filter_{dest}(\beta'_d, d), s)$

then the following theorems can be used to prove (US):

(T1.1) $Project(Y_d,s) \leq Strip_{dest}(S_2)$

(T1.2) $Project(X_s,d) \geq Strip_{source}(S_1)$

These will be proved later.

Proof of (US) using (T1.1) and (T1.2):

Lemma 1.1: $User\_data\_only(Strip_{source}(S)) = User\_data\_only(Strip_{dest}(S))$

where S is a sequence of protocol data. The lemma is intuitively obvious, as the function $User\_data\_only$ discards the remaining address field of all the elements in the sequence, while leaving the user data field untouched. With this lemma, the proof is straightforward as follows:

$User\_data\_only(Project(Y_d,s)) \leq User\_data\_only(Strip_{dest}(S_2))$
          by (T1.1)
$\rightarrow User\_data\_only(Project(Y_d,s)) \leq User\_data\_only(Strip_{dest}(S_1))$
          by $S_2 \leq S_1$ from (S1.2)

$$\to User\_data\_only(Project(Y_d,s)) \lesssim User\_data\_only(Strip_{source}(S_1))$$
$$\quad\quad \text{by Lemma 1.1}$$
$$\to User\_data\_only(Project(Y_d,s)) \lesssim User\_data\_only(Project(X_s,d))$$
$$\quad\quad \text{by (T1.2)}$$

Notice that the proof above uses the sequence order-preserving properties of the functions *User_data_only* and *Strip*. Furthermore, these functions only discard *some* fields from the elements of a sequence, while *not* removing any element completely from the sequence.
Q.E.D.

Theorems (T1.1) and (T1.2) will now be proved in the following paragraphs.

$$(T1.1) \quad Project(Y_d,s) \lesssim Strip_{dest}(S_2)$$

Proof: The proof will use a small lemma:

Lemma 1.2: $Z = Strip_{dest}(\gamma) \to Project(Z,s) = Strip_{dest}(Filter_{source}(\gamma,s))$

where γ is a sequence of protocol data, i.e. the *Project* function on a sequence of data *received* by a user is 'equivalent', in some sense, to the $Filter_{source}$ function on a sequence of protocol data. More precisely, it says that all the data received by a user with a given source station address must be from the protocol data with the same source address. The proof of the lemma is trivial from the definition of the functions. So let:

$$Z = Strip_{dest}(Filter_{dest}(\beta'_d,d))$$
$$\{ \text{ i.e. } \gamma = Filter_{dest}(\beta'_d,d)) \}$$

then:

$$Y_d \lesssim Z \quad\quad\quad\quad\quad \text{by (S1.1)}$$
$$\to Project(Y_d,s) \lesssim Project(Z,s)$$
$$\to Project(Y_d,s) \lesssim Strip_{dest}(Filter_{source}(Filter_{dest}(\beta'_d,d),s))$$
$$\quad\quad \text{by Lemma 1.2}$$
$$\to Project(Y_d,s) \lesssim Strip_{dest}(S_2)$$
$$\quad\quad \text{by the definition of } S_2$$

Q.E.D.

$$(T1.2) \quad Project(X_s,d) \gtrsim Strip_{source}(S_1)$$

Proof: The proof here is very similar to that of (T1.1), using the lemma:

Lemma 1.3: $Z = Strip_{source}(\gamma) \to Project(Z,d) = Strip_{source}(Filter_{dest}(\gamma,d))$

where γ is a sequence of protocol data, i.e. the *Project* function on a sequence of information *sent* by a user is 'equivalent' in some sense to the $Filter_{dest}$ function on a sequence of protocol data.
With:

$$Z = Strip_{source}(\alpha'_s)$$

we have:

$$X_s \geqslant Z \qquad \text{by (S1.3)}$$
$$\rightarrow\ Project(X_s, d) \geqslant Project(Z, d)$$
$$\rightarrow\ Project(X_s, d) \geqslant Strip_{source}(Filter_{dest}(\alpha'_s, d))$$
$$\text{by Lemma 1.3}$$
$$\rightarrow\ Project(X_s, d) \geqslant Strip_{source}(S_1)$$
$$\text{by definition of } S_1$$

Q.E.D.

Notice that the proofs of (T1.1) and (T1.2) use the order preserving property of the function *Project*.

Finally, the refinement on the liveness property (UL1) can be verified easily as follows:

$$\text{(UL1)} \qquad [SEND_s(d, m)] \Diamond\ AVAILABLE_d (s, m)$$

Proof:

$$[SEND_s(d, m)] \Diamond \text{obl}(PUT_s(p))$$
$$\text{where } Source\_id\_of(p) = s$$
$$\text{and } Dest\_id\_of(p) = d$$
$$\text{and } Msg\_of(p) = m \qquad\qquad \text{by (L1.1)}$$
$$\rightarrow\ [SEND_s(d, m)] \Diamond ARRIVE_d (p) \qquad \text{by (L1.2)}$$
$$\rightarrow\ [SEND_s(d, m)] \Diamond AVAILABLE_d (s, m)$$
$$\qquad\qquad\qquad\qquad \text{by (L1.3) (L1.4) \& (L1.5)}$$
Q.E.D.

3.5.3.2   *Step 2*

The task of this step is simply to identify the reason for data collision on the ring, then to make a first step towards preventing its happening. In other words, this step is aimed at implementing (L1.2) and (S1.2) using the properties of the underlying medium.

(1) Refinement   To make sure that (S1.2) and (L1.2) are satisfied, it will be interesting to examine the property, (ML1), of the underlying medium being used, which states that if no collision occurs after a message has been dispatched on to the ring, then it will be able to reach the remaining stations on the ring intact. The method for providing a reliable service is then to make sure that no collision will ever occur. The reason for collision is that the message from some other station arrives at a station at such a time that it coincides with an event in which data are output from that station. So collision prevention basically means that no message arrives at a station during the time the station is transmitting, as specified by the following axiom:

$$\text{(S2.5)} \qquad \text{permit}(PUT_s) \rightarrow \neg\exists\, m\ .\ <T> ARRIVE_s (m)$$

where T is the duration of operation PUT.

It is assumed that the constant T is the maximum duration of the executions of all PUT operations, so (S2.5) is a rather strong precaution against possible data collision. All the safety axioms from step 1 are retained as (S2.1)–(S2.4).

The liveness axioms (L1.3)–(L1.6) are retained as (L2.3)–(L2.6) respectively, while (L1.1) is refined by:

$$(L2.1) \quad [SEND_s(dest,m)] \Diamond (permit(PUT_s)$$
$$\rightarrow obl(PUT_s(data(s, dest, m))))$$

i.e. data from the user will be sent down the ring once the station has got permission to transmit. (L1.2) is replaced by a more concrete version (cf. (ML1) of the medium):

$$(L2.2) \quad [PUT_s(p)] \; O(T_{s,d})ARRIVE_d(p)$$
$$\text{where } d = Dest\_id\_of(p)$$

To ensure that each station *will* have permission to transmit, the following liveness axiom is added:

$$(L2.7) \quad \forall s . \Box \Diamond \; permit(PUT_s)$$

So the listing of the step 2 specification is as shown below:

Safety

$$(S2.1) \quad Y_d \lesssim Strip_{dest}(Filter_{dest}(Protocol\_data\_only(\beta_d),d))$$
$$(S2.2) \quad Filter_{source}(Filter_{dest}(\beta_d,d),s) \leqslant Filter_{dest}(\alpha_s,d)$$
$$(S2.3) \quad Strip_{source}(Protocol\_data\_only(\alpha_s)) \leqslant X_s$$
$$(S2.4) \quad data(s\_id, d\_id, m) \in \alpha_s \rightarrow s\_id = s$$
$$(S2.5) \quad permit(PUT_s) \rightarrow \neg \exists m . <T> ARRIVE_s(m)$$

where *T* is the duration of operation *PUT*.

Liveness

$$(L2.1) \quad [SEND_s(dest,m)] \Diamond (permit(PUT_s)$$
$$\rightarrow obl(PUT_s(data(s, dest, m))))$$

$$(L2.2) \quad [PUT_s(p)] \; O(T_{s,d})ARRIVE_d(p)$$
$$\text{where } d = Dest\_id\_of(p)$$
$$(L2.3) \quad ARRIVE_d(p) \rightarrow obl(GET_d)$$
$$(L2.4) \quad ARRIVE_d(p') \text{ During } GET_d(p) \rightarrow [GET_d(p)]p = p'$$
$$(L2.5) \quad [GET_d(p)] \; (Dest\_id\_of(p) = d$$
$$\rightarrow \Diamond AVAILABLE_d(s\_id,m))$$
$$\text{where } s\_id = Source\_id\_of(p) \text{ and } m = Msg\_of(p)$$
$$(L2.6) \quad AVAILABLE_d(s',m') \text{ During } RECEIVE_d(s,m)$$
$$\rightarrow [RECEIVE_d(s,m)] \; (m = m' \land s = s')$$
$$(L2.7) \quad \forall s . \Box \Diamond \; permit(PUT_s)$$

(2) Further refinement needed   It is apparent that (S2.5) is not totally localised yet, because the arrival of a message is under the control not of the target station, but of the station which sends the message. So a localised control is needed to implement (S2.5).

(L2.7) appears to be local, as it has only a single service primitive involved, but to achieve it while preserving (S2.5) (collision avoidance) needs careful refinement work, by exerting local discipline on each protocol entity.

(3) Verification   The most important property introduced by the refinement in this step is that data collision will not occur, which can be stated by the following theorem:

(T2.1) $\forall s$. $\Box\neg COLLISION\,(s)$

Proof:

$\forall s$. $\text{permit}(PUT_s)$
$\rightarrow \neg\exists m$. $<T>\ ARRIVE_s(m)$ by (S2.5)
$\rightarrow \neg COLLISION\,(s)$

by the definition of *COLLISION*. As (S2.5) is a tautology, i.e. it holds throughout the operation of the system, so we have:

$\forall s$. $\Box\neg COLLISION\,(s)$

Q.E.D.

The proof of (L1.1), which has been replaced in this step, is also very straightforward, as shown below.

(L1.1) $[SEND_s\,(dest,\ m)]\ \diamondsuit\ \text{obl}(PUT_s(\text{data}(s\ ,\ ,dest,\ m))$

Proof:

$[SEND_s(d\,,m\,)]\ \diamondsuit\ (\text{permit}(PUT_s)\ \rightarrow\ \text{obl}(PUT_s(p)))$
$\qquad\qquad\qquad\text{where } Source\_id\_of(p)\!=\!s$
$\qquad\qquad\qquad\text{and } Dest\_id\_of(p)\!=\!d$
$\qquad\qquad\qquad\text{and } Msg\_of(p)\!=\!m$
$\qquad\qquad\text{by (L2.1)}$
$\rightarrow [SEND_s(d\,,m\,)]\ (\diamondsuit\ \text{permit}(PUT_s)\ \rightarrow \diamondsuit\ \text{obl}(PUT_s(p)))$
$\qquad\qquad\text{by the distributivity property of}\diamondsuit$
$\rightarrow [SEND_s(d\,,m\,)]\ \diamondsuit\ \text{obl}(PUT_s(p))$
$\qquad\qquad\text{by (L2.7)}$

Q.E.D.

3.5.3.3 Step 3
The emphasis of this step is on refining (S2.5), one of the two non-local axioms from the last step, using information in the time taken for a message travelling from one station to another.

(1) Refinement   The intuitive idea of the refinement here is that if a station is permitted to transmit, then no other station is allowed to transmit in a period of time beforehand which might cause collision. Formally, (S2.5) is replaced by:

(S3.5) $ARRIVE_s\,(m)$
$\qquad\qquad\rightarrow \exists m'$. $\exists d\neq s$. $O(\text{-}T_{d,s})\,(true\ \textbf{During}\ PUT_s(m'))$

The above axiom, in fact, simply states the property of the medium (MS2), which says that any message travelling in the ring must be sent by one of the stations on the ring.

(S3.6) $\text{permit}(PUT_s) \rightarrow \forall d \neq s . [-T_{d,s}] \neg\text{permit}(PUT_d)$

Recall that $T_{d,s}$ is the time taken for a message travelling from station d to station s. It is assumed that the duration of the execution of the *PUT* operation is negligible compared with the time taken for a message moving from one station to another. The liveness properties are left untouched. So the resulting axioms of step 3 are:

Safety

(S3.1) $Y_d \leqslant Strip_{dest}(Filter_{dest}(Protocol\_data\_only(\beta_d),d))$
(S3.2) $Filter_{source}(Filter_{dest}(\beta_d,d),s) \leqslant Filter_{dest}(\alpha_s,d)$
(S3.3) $Strip_{source}(Protocol\_data\_only(\alpha_s)) \leqslant X_s$
(S3.4) $data(s\_id, d\_id, m) \in \alpha_s \rightarrow s\_id = s$

(S3.5) $ARRIVE_s(m)$
         $\rightarrow \exists m' . \exists d \neq s . O(-T_{d,s}) (true \text{ During } PUT_s(m'))$
(S3.6) $\text{permit}(PUT_s) \rightarrow \forall d \neq s . [-T_{d,s}] \neg\text{permit}(PUT_d)$

Liveness

(L3.1) $[SEND_s(dest,m)] \diamondsuit (\text{permit}(PUT_s)$
         $\rightarrow \text{obl}(PUT_s(data(s, dest, m))))$

(L3.2) $[PUT_s(p)] O(T_{s,d})ARRIVE_d(p)$
         where $d = Dest\_id\_of(p)$
(L3.3) $ARRIVE_d(p) \rightarrow \text{obl}(GET_d)$
(L3.4) $ARRIVE_d(p') \text{ During } GET_d(p) \rightarrow [GET_d(p)]p = p'$
(L3.5) $[GET_d(p)] (Dest\_id\_of(p) = d$
         $\rightarrow \diamondsuit AVAILABLE_d(s\_id, m))$
         where $s\_id = Source\_id\_of(p)$
         and $m = Msg\_of(p)$
(L3.6) $AVAILABLE_d(s', m') \text{ During } RECEIVE_d(s, m)$
         $\rightarrow [RECEIVE_d(s, m)] (m = m' \wedge s = s')$
(L3.7) $\forall s . \square \diamondsuit \text{permit}(PUT_s)$

(2) Further refinement needed   (S3.5) is supported by the medium's property (MS2). So only (S3.6) and (L3.7) need further refinement, because (S3.6) has service primitives not local to the same protocol entity, while (L3.7) is a non-local axiom retained from the last step.

(3) Verification   Only (S2.5) needs to be verified.

(S2.5) $\text{permit}(PUT_s) \rightarrow \neg\exists m . <T> ARRIVE_s(m)$

where T is the duration of operation *PUT*.

Proof:
         $\text{permit}(PUT_s)$
         $\rightarrow \forall d \neq s . [-T_{d,s}] \neg\text{permit}(PUT_d)$
         by (S3.6)

$$\rightarrow \forall\, d \neq s\,.\,[-T_{d,s}]\neg\exists\, m\,.\,(\textit{true}\ \textbf{During}\ PUT_s(m))$$
$$\text{by the property of }\textbf{permit}$$
$$\rightarrow \forall\, d \neq s\,.\,[-T_{d,s}]\neg\exists\, m\,.\,O(T_{d,s})\ ARRIVE_s(m)$$
$$\text{by (S3.5)}$$
$$\rightarrow \forall\, d \neq s\,.\,\neg\exists\, m\,.\,[-T_{d,s}]\ O(T_{d,s})\ ARRIVE_s(m)$$
$$\text{by temporal property (p11) (see section 5.2.3)}$$
$$\rightarrow \forall\, d \neq s\,.\,\neg\exists\, m\,.\,[T_{d,s}]\ ARRIVE_s(m)$$
$$\text{by temporal property (p15) (see section 5.2.3)}$$
$$\rightarrow \neg\exists\, m\,.\,[T]\ ARRIVE_s(m)$$
$$\text{where } T \text{ is equal to the duration of } PUT$$
$$\text{by the assumption that } T \ll T_{d,s}$$

Q.E.D.

3.5.3.4 *Step 4*

The task of this step is to use the token passing scheme to 'implement' (S3.6), which is the safety requirement on data collision avoidance. The other non-local axiom, (L3.7), is not addressed in this step.

(1) Refinement   The idea of token passing is a very simple one. It means that only the station possessing the token is allowed to transmit its message(s), while the remaining stations listen to the ring. There is only one token circulating around the ring, so it is guaranteed to have only one station transmitting at a time, thus eliminating the possibility of data collision.

Since the token is circulated by means of the message passing mechanism, by examining the history variables associated with a station for accessing the medium, it is possible to tell if it has the token or not. If the station has the token, it means that the token has been received but not yet passed on to the next station. In other words, there is a token addressed to it in its input history variable, β, and there is no token in its output history variable α that is recorded later than the one in β.

To talk about the temporal relationship between message passing events which are recorded in separate history variables, the easiest way forward is to use the notion of *time stamp*. This means using an imaginary device that stamps the current time on a message when it is recorded in its history variable. So the function:

   Time_stamp(msg)

returns the time at which *msg* is sent (or received).

To identify the last token in a history variable, the function *last_token* is introduced, so that:

   last_token(α)

returns the latest token recorded in the message history variable α.

The protocol entity will now use a protocol control packet called TOKEN, where TOKEN is of the format:

   TOKEN(*s*: **Station_Id**)

With the above preparation, the actual refinement is given by replacing (S3.6) with:

(S4.6)   **permit**(PUT_s) $\longleftrightarrow$ *Has_token*(s)

i.e. making **permit**(PUT_s) and *Has_token*(s) synonymous. And *Has_token* is defined in terms of history variables:

(S4.7) $Has\_token(s)$
$\longleftrightarrow last\_token(\beta_s) = \text{TOKEN}(s)$
$\wedge\ (\exists s'\ .\ \text{TOKEN}(s')\in\alpha_s$
$\rightarrow Time\_stamp(last\_token(\beta_s))$
$< Time\_stamp(last\_token(\alpha_s)))$

Notice that there is no need to make a real time stamping mechanism. For a program to realize the above axiom, it only needs to keep track of when it receives the last token, and when the token is passed on to the next station.

(S4.8) $\text{TOKEN}(d)\in\alpha_s\ \rightarrow\ d\neq s$

i.e. a station cannot pass the token to itself.

(S4.9) $Has\_token(s)\ \rightarrow\ \forall\ d\neq s\ .\ \neg Has\_token(d)$

i.e. no two stations can have the token at the same time.

With the definition of *Has_token* given, **permit**(PUT_s) is replaced by *Has_token*(s) in the rest of the step 3 axioms, resulting in the following step 4 axioms:

Safety

(S4.1) $Y_d \lesssim Strip_{dest}(Filter_{dest}(Protocol\_data\_only(\beta_d),d))$
(S4.2) $Filter_{source}(Filter_{dest}(\beta_d,d),s) \lesssim Filter_{dest}(\alpha_s,d)$
(S4.3) $Strip_{source}(Protocol\_data\_only(\alpha_s)) \lesssim X_s$
(S4.4) $data(s\_id,\ d\_id,\ m)\in\alpha_s\ \rightarrow\ s\_id = s$
(S4.5) $ARRIVE(m)$
$\rightarrow \exists m'\ .\ \exists\ d\neq s\ .\ O(-T_{d,s})\ (true\ \textbf{During}\ PUT_s(m'))$
(S4.6)   **permit**(PUT_s) $\longleftrightarrow$ *Has_token*(s)
(S4.7) $Has\_token(s)$
$\longleftrightarrow last\_token(\beta_s) = \text{TOKEN}(s)$
$\wedge\ (\exists s'\ .\ \text{TOKEN}(s')\in\alpha_s$
$\rightarrow Time\_stamp(last\_token(\beta_s))$
$< Time\_stamp(last\_token(\alpha_s)))$
(S4.8) $\text{TOKEN}(d)\in\alpha_s\ \rightarrow\ d\neq s$
(S4.9) $Has\_token(s)\ \rightarrow\ \forall\ d\neq s\ .\ \neg Has\_token(d)$

Liveness

(L4.1) $[SEND_s(dest,m)]\ \diamondsuit\ (Has\_token(s)$
$\rightarrow obl(PUT_s(data(s,\ dest,\ m))))$
(L4.2) $[PUT_s(p)]\ O(T_{s,d})ARRIVE_d\ (p)$
where $d = Dest\_id\_of(p)$
(L4.3) $ARRIVE_d\ (p)\ \rightarrow\ obl(GET_d)$
(L4.4) $ARRIVE_d\ (p')\ \textbf{During}\ GET_d\ (p)$
$\rightarrow [GET_d(p)]p = p$

(L4.5) $[GET_d(p)]$ $(Dest\_id\_of(p)=d$
          $\rightarrow \diamondsuit AVAILABLE_d(s\_id,m))$
          where $s\_id = Source\_id\_of(p)$
          and $m = Msg\_of(p)$
(L4.6) $AVAILABLE_d(s',m')$ **During** $RECEIVE_d(s,m)$
          $\rightarrow [RECEIVE_d(s,m)]$ $(m=m' \wedge s=s')$
(L4.7) $\forall s . \Box \diamondsuit Has\_token(s)$

(2) Further refinement needed   (S4.9) is obviously not yet localised, as it has predicates associated with more than one protocol entity. (L4.7), a non-local axiom resulting from the last step, still waits to be refined.

(3) Verification   The goal of the verification is to show that:

(S3.6)   **permit**(PUT_s) $\rightarrow \forall d \neq s$. $[-T_{d,s}]$ ¬**permit**(PUT_d)

is satisfied by the step 4 axioms. With (S4.6), it is equivalent to show that:

(S3.6*) $Has\_token(s)$ $\rightarrow \forall d \neq s$. $[-T_{d,s}]$ ¬$Has\_token(d)$

Proof: Diagrammatically, (S4.7)–(S4.9) only allow the situation depicted in Fig. 3.11 to take place. Notice that the leading edge of each *Has_token* interval corresponds to the receipt of a token addressed to the owning station, and the rear edge corresponds to the event of passing on the token to the next station. These properties are supported by (S4.7). (S3.6) obviously holds if the claim pictured in Fig. 3.11 is true.

To support the claim depicted in Fig. 3.11, it is necessary to show that there is no overlapping of time intervals for two stations having the token, i.e. the situation depicted in Fig. 3.12 cannot happen. However, (S4.9) denies the chance for this to happen.

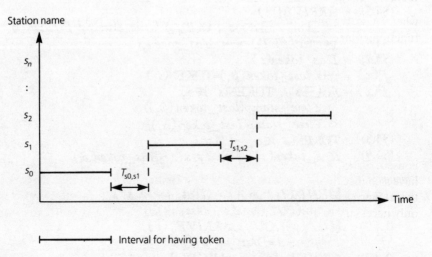

Fig. 3.11 Demonstration for token passing algorithm.

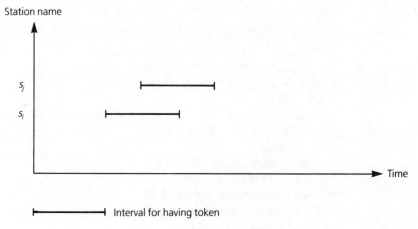

Fig. 3.12 Overlapping token possession.

3.5.3.5 *Step 5*

The objective of the step is to ensure that every station will have its fair chance to transmit, i.e. every station will periodically have the token. The remaining non-local axioms (L4.7) and (S4.9) will be dealt with here.

(1) Refinement   To avoid a station holding on to the token forever, a new liveness axiom (L5.7) is used to replace (L4.7):

(L5.7) $Has\_token(s) \rightarrow \diamond \; obl(PUT_s(TOKEN(Next\_station \; (s))))$

To make sure that token passing is fair, the function *Next_station*, which is known to every station, must have the following property:

(S5.10) $\forall \, s,d \in \textbf{Station\_Id} \; . \; \exists \, n \leqslant N \; \wedge \; Next\_station^n(s) = d$

where N is the number of stations on the ring. Here, the convention on function composition:

$$f^0(x) = x$$
$$f^1(x) = f(x)$$
$$f^2(x) = f(f(x))$$
$$\vdots$$
$$\vdots$$
$$f^n(x) = f(f^{n-1}(x))$$

is used. So (S5.10) together with (L5.7) ensures that all other stations will have a chance to have the token before a particular station can have the token twice. Since each station has a unique identifier, so to implement (S4.9), it is only necessary to replace it by:

(S5.9)   **Initially** $\exists \, !s \; . \; Has\_token(s)$

i.e. when the network first starts operation, there is a unique station which assumes the token. The resultant specification of this step is listed below:

Safety

(S5.1) $Y_d \lesssim Strip_{dest}(Filter_{dest}(Protocol\_data\_only(\beta_d),d))$

(S5.2) $Filter_{source}(Filter_{dest}(\beta_d,d),s) \leqslant Filter_{dest}(\alpha_s,d)$

(S5.3) $Strip_{source}(Protocol\_data\_only(\alpha_s)) \leqslant X_s$

(S5.4) $data(s\_id, d\_id, m) \in \alpha_s \rightarrow s\_id = s$

(S5.5) $ARRIVE_s(m)$
$\rightarrow \exists m' . \exists d \neq s . \bigcirc(-T_{d,s}) (true \textbf{ During } PUT_s(m'))$

(S5.6) $\textbf{permit}(PUT_s) \longleftrightarrow Has\_token(s)$

(S5.7) $Has\_token(s)$
$\longleftrightarrow last\_token(\beta_s) = TOKEN(s)$
$\wedge (\exists s' . TOKEN(s') \in \alpha_s$
$\rightarrow Time\_stamp(last\_token(\beta_s))$
$< Time\_stamp(last\_token(\alpha_s)))$

(S5.8) $TOKEN(d) \in \alpha_s \rightarrow d \neq s$

(S5.9)   Initially $\exists ! s . Has\_token(s)$

(S510) $\forall s,d \in \textbf{Station\_Id} . \exists n \leqslant N \wedge Next\_station^n(s) = d$

where N is the number of stations on the ring.

Liveness

(L5.1) $[SEND_s(dest,m)] \diamondsuit (Has\_token(s)$
$\rightarrow \text{obl}(PUT_s(data(s, dest, m))))$

(L5.2) $[PUT_s(p)] \bigcirc(T_{s,d}) ARRIVE_d(p)$
     where $d = Dest\_id\_of(p)$

(L5.3) $ARRIVE_d(p) \rightarrow \text{obl}(GET_d)$

(L5.4) $ARRIVE_d(p') \textbf{ During } GET_d(p) \rightarrow [GET_d(p)]p = p'$

(L5.5) $[GET_d(p)] (Dest\_id\_of(p) = d$
$\rightarrow \diamondsuit AVAILABLE_d(s\_id,m))$
     where $s\_id = Source\_id\_of(p)$
     and $m = Msg\_of(p)$

(L5.6) $AVAILABLE_d(s',m') \textbf{ During } RECEIVE_d(s,m)$
$\rightarrow [RECEIVE_d(s,m)] (m = m' \wedge s = s')$

(L5.7) $Has\_token(s) \rightarrow \diamondsuit \text{obl}(PUT_s(TOKEN(Next\_station(s))))$

(2) Further refinement needed   All the axioms given in this step can either be realised locally, or are directly supported by the underlying medium, so all one needs to do next is to identify those axioms corresponding to any station (or the underlying medium).

Notice that *Next_station*, which is defined in (S5.10), can be considered as a global function, but once it is formally defined each station must have a local copy of it, i.e. it is a commonly agreed function.

(3) Verification

(S4.9) $Has\_token(s) \rightarrow \forall d \neq s . \neg Has\_token(d)$

Proof: It can be proved by induction on time.
    i) Base case: Initially (S4.9) is true by (S5.9).

ii) Induction step: Intuitively, the emphasis is on showing that if (S4.9) is true when a station, *s* say, has the token, then (S4.9) will still hold true after *s* passes the token on to the next station. This is intuitively trivial to show, because each station has a unique identifier, so there will only be *one* station that can have the token next. A sketch of the formal proof is the following:

$$\text{Assuming } Has\_token(s) \land \forall d \neq s . \neg Has\_token(d)$$

$$Has\_token(s) \land obl(PUT_s(TOKEN(Next\_station\ (s))))$$
$$\land\ \forall d' \neq s . \neg Has\_token(d')$$
$$\rightarrow \exists !d \in \text{Station\_Id} . d = Next\_station(s)$$
$$\land\ [T_{s,d}] \neg \exists d' \in \text{Station\_Id} . Has\_token(d')$$
$$\land\ O(T_{s,d}+1)\ (Has\_token(d) \land \forall d' \neq d . \neg Has\_token(d'))$$
$$\text{by (S5.7) and (L5.2)}$$
$$\rightarrow O(T_{s,d}+1)\ (Has\_token(d) \rightarrow \forall d' \neg = s . \neg Has\_token(d'))$$

Q.E.D.

(L4.7) $\forall s . \Box \Diamond\ Has\_token(s)$

Proof:

Initially $\exists !d . Has\_token(d)$ by (S5.9)

$$\rightarrow \Diamond\ obl(PUT_s(TOKEN(Next\_station\ (d)))) \qquad \text{by (L5.7)}$$
$$\rightarrow \Diamond\Diamond\ ARRIVE_d\ (TOKEN(Next\_station\ (d))) \qquad \text{by (L5.2)}$$
$$\rightarrow \Diamond\ ARRIVE_d\ (TOKEN(Next\_station\ (d))) \qquad \text{by property of} \Diamond$$
$$\rightarrow \Diamond\ Has\_token(Next\_station(d)) \qquad \text{by (L5.3) (L5.4) \& (S5.7)}$$
$$\vdots$$
$$\vdots \quad \{n\text{-1 steps later}\}$$
$$\vdots$$
$$\rightarrow \exists n \leqslant N . (\Diamond Has\_token(s)) \land s = Next\_station^n(d) \qquad \text{by (S5.10)}$$

where N = number of stations on the ring. This is the first time that the token is circulated in the ring. But for later rounds, similar proofs can be performed. So we have:

$$\forall s . \Box \Diamond\ Has\_token(s)$$

Q.E.D.

3.5.3.6   Step 6
This is where the local axioms of a protocol entity are identified. Since each station is identical in providing the service, it is enough to describe the specification for one of them, the one in station *s*, say.

(1) Protocol entity specification   For the protocol entity in station *s*, its specification is as follows, with its external view depicted in Fig. 3.13.

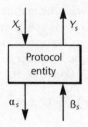

Fig. 3.13 External view of the protocol entity at station *s*.

Service primitive operations provided to the user

$SEND_s$ (*dest_adrs*: **Station_Id**; *msg*: **User_Data_Unit**)
  $X=A$ →
  [$SEND_s$(*dest*,*msg*)]$X=A$ <(*dest*,*msg*)>

$RECEIVE_s$(**var** *d*: **Station_Id**; **var** *m*: **User_Data_Unit**)
  $Y_s=B$ →
  [$RECEIVE_s$(*d*,*m*)] ∃ *s*',*m*' . ($Y=B$ <(*s*',*m*')>) ∧ *d*=*s*' ∧ *m*=*m*')

Here *A* and *B* are assumed to be some sequence constants.

Definitions of data types and functions   The data types and functions introduced during the refinement are very important, since without them the specification is not very useful.

Data type   The type of data acceptable by the medium is called **Packet**, with two sub-types:

  Packet = Protocol_Data_Unit + Protocol_Control_Unit

The formats of the sub-types are as follows:

Protocol_Data_Unit
      = data(*source*, *dest*: **Station_Id**; *msg*: **User_Data_Unit**)
Protocol_Control_Unit = TOKEN(*s*: **Station_Id**)

Auxiliary functions   Firstly, some functions on protocol data are given as follows:

  Source_id_of: **Protocol_Data_Unit** → **Station_Id**
  /* Returns the source address of a data item */
  —*Source_id_of*(data(*s* ,*d* ,*m*))=*s*

  Dest_id_of: **Protocol_Data_Unit** → **Station_Id**
  /* Returns the destination address of a data item */
  —*Dest_id_of*(data(*s* ,*d* ,*m*))=*d*

  Msg_of: **Protocol_Data_Unit** → **User_Data_Unit**
  /* Returns the user message in the data item */
  —*Msg_of*(data(*s* ,*d* ,*m*))=*m*

The following functions are on protocol data sequences:

Protocol_data_only: *Sequence of* **Packet**
$\rightarrow$ *Sequence of* **Protocol_Data_Unit**
/* Extract the sequence of protocol data (discarding protocol controls) from a given sequence of **Packets** */
——*Protocol_data_only*(P)=P'
   Where $P' \lesssim P$
     and $\forall\, d \in P$. d is **Protocol_Data_Unit** $\rightarrow$ $d \in P'$
     and $\forall\, d \in P'$. $Count(P',d)$=$Count(P,d)$

Filter$_{source}$: *Sequence of* (**Protocol_Data_Unit** , **Station_Id**)
            $\rightarrow$ *Sequence of* **Protocol_Data_Unit**
/* Returns the sequence of protocol data with the given source address   */
——*Filter$_{source}$*(P,s)=P'
   where $P' \lesssim P$
     and $\forall\, m \in P'$. $Source\_id\_of(m)$=s
     and $\forall\, m \in P'$. $Count(P',m)$=$Count(P,m)$

Filter$_{dest}$: *Sequence of* (**Protocol_Data_Unit** , **Station_Id**)
            $\rightarrow$ *Sequence of* **Protocol_Data_Unit**
/* Returns the sequence of protocol data with the given destination address   */
——*Filter$_{dest}$*(P,d)=P'
   where $P' \lesssim P$
     and $\forall\, m \in P'$. $Dest\_id\_of(m)$=s
     and $\forall\, m \in P'$. $Count(P',m)$=$Count(P,m)$

Strip$_{source}$: *Sequence of* **Protocol_Data_Unit**
            $\rightarrow$ *Sequence of* (**Station_Id, User_Data_Unit**)
/* Maps a sequence of protocol data to the corresponding one that are *sent* by a user   */
——*Strip$_{source}$*$(<S\_id_i,D\_id_i,m_i>_{i=1}^n)$=$<D\_id_i,m_i>_{i=1}^k$

Strip$_{dest}$: *Sequence of* **Protocol_Data_Unit**
            $\rightarrow$ *Sequence of* (**Station_Id, User_Data_Unit**)
/* Maps a sequence of protocol data to the corresponding one that are *received* by a user   */
——*Strip$_{dest}$*$(<S\_id_i,D\_id_i,m_i>_{i=1}^n)$=$<S\_id_i,m_i>_{i=1}^k$

Furthermore, each station has an identical copy of the function *Next_station*, which satisfies the axiom:

(S5.10) $\forall\, d,s \in$ **Station_Id** . $\exists\, n \leq N \wedge Next\_station^n(s)$=$d$

where N = the number of stations on the ring.

Behavioural specification   For each station, *s*, on the ring, we have the following axioms:

Safety

(S1) $Y_d \leq Strip_{dest}(Filter_{dest}(Protocol\_data\_only(\beta_d),d))$
        This is (S5.1)

(S2) $Strip_{source}(Protocol\_data\_only(\alpha_s)) \leq X_s$
        This is (S5.3)

(S3)   data(s_id , d_id , m)$\in \alpha_s$ → $s\_id = s$
        This is (S5.4)

(S4)   **permit**(PUT_s) ⟷ $Has\_token(s)$
        This is (S5.6)

(S5) $Has\_token(s)$
        ⟷ $last\_token(\beta_s) = TOKEN(s)$
        $\wedge$ ($\exists s'$. $TOKEN(s') \in \alpha_s$
        → $Time\_stamp(last\_token(\beta_s))$
        < $Time\_stamp(last\_token(\alpha_s)))$
        This is (S5.7)

(S6) $TOKEN(d) \in \alpha_s$ → $d \neq s$
        This is (S5.8)

Liveness

(L1) $[SEND_s(dest,m)] \diamondsuit (Has\_token(s)$
        → obl(PUT_s(data(s , $dest$, m))))
        This is (L5.1)

(L2) $ARRIVE_d(p)$ → obl(GET_d)
        This is (L5.3)

(L3) $ARRIVE_d(p')$ **During** $GET_d(p)$ → $[GET_d(p)]p=p'$
        This is (L5.4)

(L4) $[GET_d(p)](Dest\_id\_of(p)=d$ → $\diamondsuit AVAILABLE_d(s\_id,m))$
        where $s\_id = Source\_id\_of(p)$
        and $m = Msg\_of(p)$
        This is (L5.5)

(L5) $AVAILABLE_d(s',m')$ **During** $RECEIVE_d(s,m)$
        → $[RECEIVE_d(s,m)]$ ($m=m'$ $\wedge$ $s=s'$)
        This is (L5.6)

(L6) $Has\_token(s)$ → $\diamondsuit$obl (PUT_s(TOKEN(Next_station (s))))
        This is (L5.7)

For the station, call it s_0, which has the token at the very beginning of the operation of the network, there is an additional axiom:

(S0)   Initially $Has\_token(s_0)$

which is in fact (S5.9), saying that station s_0 assumes the token at the very beginning of the operation of the network.

(2) Properties of the medium   The remaining axioms (S5.2) (S5.5) and (L5.2) are supported by the service provided by the medium, with the help of:

(T2.1) $\forall s \in$ **Station_Id** . $\square \neg COLLISION(s)$

which is proved in step 2.

More specifically, we have

$$(MS2) = (S5.5)$$

and

$$(T2.1) \wedge (ML1) \rightarrow (L5.2)$$

where (MS2) and (ML1) are the properties of the medium (see section 3.5.2.2).

$$(S5.2) \quad Filter_{source}(Filter_{dest}(\beta_d,d),s) \leqslant Filter_{dest}(\alpha_s,d)$$

can be proved by first showing:

$$(T6.1) \quad Filter_{dest}(Filter_{source}(\beta_d,s),d) \lesssim Filter_{dest}(\alpha_s,d)$$

Proof of (T6.1)

$$\exists \pi \in \bigcup_{s' \neq d} \alpha_{s'} \; . \; \beta_d \lesssim \pi \qquad \text{by (MS1) \& (T2.1)}$$

{see 3.2.2 for the definition of $\bigcup$ }

$$\rightarrow Filter_{source}(\beta_d,s) \lesssim Filter_{source}(\pi,s)$$

$$\rightarrow Filter_{source}(\beta_d,s) \lesssim \alpha_s$$

as protocol data with source address s can only be from α_s by (S3)

$$\rightarrow Filter_{dest}(Filter_{source}(\beta_d,s),d) \lesssim Filter_{dest}(\alpha_s,d)$$

Q.E.D.

Then to show (S5.2) holds, i.e. $\lesssim$ in (T6.1) is in fact $\leqslant$, one is left to show that every piece of data arriving at a station will be collected by the protocol entity there. This is guaranteed by axioms (L2) and (L3).

3.6 CONCLUSION

In this chapter we have presented a logic formalism for the formal *specification and verification* of protocol problems. A token passing protocol on a ring network is developed, following the top-down step-wise refinement methodology, to demonstrate the practicality of formal methods in the process of protocol design.

An important benefit of using formal methods in system specification is to eliminate ambiguities. Moreover, the formalism presented here is shown to be satisfactory, through the example, with respect to the criteria laid down at the beginning of the chapter, as follows.

3.6.1 Generality

The interests of the user as well as those of the protocol designer can be captured by the service specification and protocol specification.

The present model is aimed at expressing both *medium access control protocols*, and *data transfer protocols* [Li, 1986]. The former generally need explicit reference to time. There has not been any previous work dealing with both classes of protocols to the authors' knowledge. Most of them are for the specification of the latter type; Shasha *et al.* [Shasha *et al.*, 1983] specify a protocol (the Ethernet Carrier Sense Protocol) of the former type. Extensive examples of both types of protocol are dealt with in [Li, 1986].

3.6.2 Modularity

The proposed model can be used to accomplish modularity in specifications by expressing the behaviour of a system in terms of its *external observable operations* (service primitives) together with the message histories associated with these operations. The *internal control structure* of the system being specified can be hidden by relating the executions of its service primitives using temporal operators [Pnueli, 1977].

Many researchers have realised this point, and various *trace-models* have been proposed, see for example [Hailpern and Owicki, 1980; COSY; Nguyen *et al.*, 1985].

3.6.3 Decomposability

Many existing models for distributed computing, such as CCS [Milner, 1980] and the Kahn-MacQueen Stream Processing Model, make it almost impossible to use *step-wise refinement* in decomposing protocol service specifications into protocol entity specifications. The main reason for this difficulty is that the structure imposed on a protocol entity specification is too strict (this is partly due to the formalisms used as well), so that there is not much room left for any intermediate refinement steps.

The model described here does not impose such a restriction; a protocol can be viewed as a centralised global implementation, as well as a distributed one, of its service. It is then possible to carry out step-wise refinement during the decomposition.

3.6.4 Simplicity and intuitivity

The functionality of a protocol or a service can be directly expressed in terms of the sequences of messages input to and output from it, because its purpose is to transmit information across the network.

The use of events to model service primitives is frequently seen in protocol specifications. But one knows that not all service primitives can be seen simply as instantaneous; one example is the synchronised message receiving operation. So for some non-trivial service-primitive operations, complex encoding is required to express the service primitive in terms of a set of events. The use of *operations* in our model can directly reflect the nature of a service primitive.

Some researchers make the assumption that once a message reaches its destination site, it will *definitely* be collected by the user there. This is typically shown in the liveness specification of a reliable communication service in [Hailpern and Owicki, 1980]. However, this is not always the case in practice. A reliable communication service can only guarantee that the message sent by a user will reach the destination site, but whether it will be collected or not depends on the user there. A simple example will illustrate this point more clearly. Let us imagine that two human users communicate with each other via remote terminals, i.e. they can send a message by typing it at their local keyboard, and receive a message by reading the local monitor. Suppose one of them goes away for a cup of tea, then they can miss some messages that arrive at their terminal during their departure, because these messages have been overwritten by messages arriving later. To reflect this kind of phenomenon in liveness specifications, the notion of *event* for the arrival of a message (or the availability of a message to be collected) must be used, and message history variables cannot be used instead.

3.7 REFERENCES

Barringer, H., Kuiper, R. and Pnueli, A. (1984) *Proceedings of 16th ACM Symposium on Theory of Computing*, 'Now You Can Compose Temporal Specifications', 51–63.

Bochmann, G. (1978) 'Finite State Description of Communication Protocols', *Computer Networks*, **2**, 361–72.

Bochmann, G. and Sunshine, S. (1980) 'Formal Methods in Communication Protocol Design', *IEEE Transactions on Communications*, **4**, 624–37.

Burstall, R. M., MacQueen, D. B. and Sannella, D. T. (1980) *HOPE: an Experimental Application Language*. Edinburgh University Department of Computer Science Report CSR–62–80.

Clark, E. M. and Emerson, A. (1981) *Proceedings of the Workshop on Logics of Programs*, 'Design and Synthesis of Programming Skeletons Using Branching Time Temporal Logic', **LNCS 131**, Springer-Verlag, Yorktown Heights, N.Y.

Dixon, R. C., Strole, N.C. and Markov, J.D. (1983) 'A Token Ring Network for Local Area Data Communications', *IBM Systems Journal*, **22**, 47–62.

Farber, D. J. and Larson, K. C. (1972) *Symposium on Computer Networks*, Polytechnic of Brooklyn, 'The System Architecture of the Distributed Computer System'.

Gabbay, D. M. (1976) *Investigation in Modal and Tense Logic with Applications to Philosophy and Linguistics*, Reidel.

Goldblatt, J. (1982) *Axiomatizing the Logics of Computer Programming*, **LCNS 130**, Springer-Verlag.

Good, D. I. and Cohen, R. M. (1978) *Compconn 78*, 'Verifiable Communication Processes', 28–35.

Hailpern, B. T. (1981) 'Verifying Concurrent Processes Using Temporal Logic', **LNCS 129**, Springer-Verlag.

Hailpern, B. T. and Owicki, S. (1980) *Verifying Network Protocols Using Temporal Logic*. Stanford University Department of Computer Science Technical Report 192.

Hughes, G. E. and Creswell, M. J. (1968) *An Introduction to Modal Logic*, Methuen.

Kahn, G. and MacQueen, D. B. (1977) *IFIP77*, 'Coroutines and Network of Parallel Processes', 993–8.

Khosla, S. (1988) *PhD Thesis in Preparation*, Department of Computing, Imperial College, London.

Kroger, F. (1977) 'LAR: a Logic of Algorithmic Reasoning', *Acta Informatica*, **8**, 243–66.

Kurose, K. (1982) *Protocol Specification, Testing and Verification*, ed. Sunshine, C.,

'The Specification and Verification of a Connection Establishment Protocol Using Temporal Logic', 43–62.

Lamport, L. (1980) *Proceedings of ACM Annual Symposium on the Principles of Programming Languages*, 'Sometime is not never: on the Temporal Logic of Programs', 174–85.

Lauer, P. E., Turrigiani, P. R. and Shields, M. W. (1979) 'COSY: a System Specification Language Based on Path and Process Assumptions', *Acta Informatica*, **12**, 109–59.

Li, D. (1986) *Top-down and Step-wise Refinement of Protocol Specifications*, PhD Thesis, Department of Computing, Imperial College, London.

Liu, M. T. (1978) *Advances in Computers*, ed. Yovits, M. C., 'Distributed Computer Networks', Academic Press, New York, 163–221.

Milner, R. (1980) *A Calculus of Communicating Systems*, **LNCS 92**, Springer-Verlag.

Minsky, N. H. (1985) *Proceedings of the 8th International Conference on Software Engineering*, 'Ensuring Integrity by Adding Obligation to Privilege'.

Moszkowski, B. C. (1983) 'Reasoning about Digital Circuits', Stanford University Department of Computer Science Technical Report STAN-CS-83-970.

Needham, R. M. (1979) *Proceedings of Seventh Symposium on Operating System Principles*, 'System Aspects of the Cambridge Ring', ACM, 82–5.

Nguyen, V., Gries, D. and Owicki, S. (1985) *12th Annual ACM Symposium on Principles of Programming Languages*, 'A Model and Temporal Proof System for Network Processes', 121–31.

Owicki, S. (1979) *Program Construction*, ed. Bauer, F. L. and Broy, M., 'Specification and Verification of a Network Mail System', 198–234.

Parnas, D. L. (1977) *Proceedings of the IFIP Conference 1977*, 'The Use of Precise Specifications in the Development of Software', 861–7.

Pierce, J. (1972) 'How Far Can Data Loop Go?', *IEEE Transactions on Communications*, **COM-20**, 512–80.

Pnueli, A. (1977) *18th Annual Symposium on Foundations of Computer Science*, 'The Temporal Logic of Programs'.

Pratt, V. R. (1976) *Proceedings of 17th Annual IEEE Symposium on Foundations of Computer Science*, 'Semantic Considerations on Floyd-Hoare Logic', 109–21.

Rudin, I. (1982) *Protocol Specification, Testing and Verification*, ed. Sunshine, C., 'Protocol Design Rules', 283–300.

Shasha, D. E., Pnueli, A. and Ewald, W. (1983) 'Temporal Verification of Carrier-Sense Local Area Network Protocols', IBM Research Division Report RC 10132 (# 45038), San Jose, Yorktown, Zurich, 8–25.

Stark, E. W. (1984) 'Foundations of a Theory of Specification for Distributed Systems', MIT Laboratory for Computer Science Technical Report 342.

Stenning, V. N. (1976) 'A Data Transfer Protocol', *Computer Networks*, **1**, 98–110.

Sunshine, C. (1979) 'Formal Techniques for Protocol Specification and Verification', *Computer Magazine*, **12**, 20–27.

Thomason, R. H. (1970) *Philosophical Problems in Logic*, ed. Labbert, K., Reidel, 'Some Completeness Results for Modal Predicate Calculi', 56–76.

Vogt, F. H. (1982) *Protocol Specification, Testing and Verification*, ed. Sunshine, C., Idyllwild, California, 'Event Based Temporal Logic Specifications of Services and Protocols', 63–74.

Wirth, N. (1971) 'Program Development by Step-wise Refinement', *Communications of the ACM*, **14**, 221–7.

Zimmerman, H. (1980) 'OSI Reference Model – the ISO Model of Architecture for Open Systems Interconnection', *IEEE Transactions on Communications*, **COM-28**, 425–32.

Chapter 4

From Specification, Through Design to Code: A Case Study in Refinement

S. KING and I. H. SØRENSEN

4.1 INTRODUCTION

In the last few years, many examples of the use of Z [King and Woodcock, 1987; Spivey, 1987; Spivey, 1988] to record specifications have been produced [Hayes, 1987; Bowen et al., 1987; Gimson, 1987]. One criticism that has been levelled at these case studies is that, despite the merits of the specification notation for recording what a system is intended to do, it is not at all clear how to get from the specification to the code which is eventually required. This activity is *refinement*, and the aim of this chapter is to give an example of a development from abstract specification through to code. It should be noted that what is presented here is *not* the only route possible from Z specification to code. While it is true that the notation and methodology for specification are well understood, there are several alternative refinement routes. The method documented here is that used by IBM UK (Hursley) [Wordsworth, 1987]. The interested reader is referred to [Morgan, 1988] for a somewhat different method, to [He et al., 1987] for the theoretical basis for refinement in Z, and to [Jones, 1986; Morris, 1987] for non-Z approaches.

This chapter is not intended as an introduction to the theory of refinement in the Z framework – see [Hoare and He, 1985]. Instead, we have tried to formalise an existing development process. At present, some developers at Hursley write their specifications in Z. Various levels of design are then recorded in Z and Dijkstra's guarded command language [Dijkstra, 1975]. We have tried to show here how to justify the designs that are recorded and to prove that the code satisfies the specification. This has not been an exercise in an entirely *formal* development. For readability, all of the proofs have been omitted, but the proof obligations are all stated – the interested reader should be able to prove any that he wishes! (A summary of proof obligations is given in 4.9.)

The system we are concerned with is described below. The specification of this system was one of the problems set for the 4th International Workshop on Software Specification and Design held in Monterey, California, in April 1987, and the statement of the problem came originally from [Kemmerer, 1985].

4.2   THE PROBLEM

Consider a small library database with the following transactions:

(1) Check out a copy of a book / Return a copy of a book;
(2) Add a copy of a book to / Remove a copy of a book from the library;
(3) Get the list of books by a particular author or in a particular subject area;
(4) Find out the list of books currently checked out by a particular borrower;
(5) Find out what borrower last checked out a particular copy of a book.

There are two types of users: staff users and ordinary borrowers. Trans-actions 1, 2, 4 and 5 are restricted to staff users, except that ordinary borrowers can perform transaction 4 to find out the list of books currently borrowed by themselves. The database must also satisfy the following constraints:

(1) All copies in the library must be available for checkout or be checked out.
(2) No copy of a book may be both available and checked out at the same time.
(3) A borrower may not have more than a predefined number of books checked out at one time.

4.3   INTERFACE DEFINITION

4.3.1   Formalisation of requirements

We address the requirements, one by one, as stated above. We introduce and derive the corresponding mathematical statements to form an incremental view of the abstract state. The first direct requirement is that 'there are two types of users: staff users and ordinary borrowers'. We assume that these two groups are distinct, that no member of staff is also an ordinary borrower.

$[PERSON]$
$staff : \mathbb{P}\, PERSON$
$borrowers : \mathbb{P}\, PERSON$
$staff \cap borrowers = \varnothing$

$PERSON$ is the set of all people that might possibly interest us.

There are three direct requirements which the database must satisfy. The first states that all copies in the library, the *stock*, must be available for checkout or checked out.

$[COPY]$
$stock : \mathbb{P}\, COPY$
$available : \mathbb{P}\, COPY$
$checked\_out : COPY \nrightarrow PERSON$
$(\mathrm{dom}\ checked\_out) \cup available = stock$

COPY is a set which contains a unique identifier for each copy of a book in the library. We represent the borrowed books by the mapping *checked_out*, which associates a book with the person who has borrowed it.

The second requirement on the database is that no copy of a book may be both available and checked out at the same time.

$$(\text{dom } checked\_out) \cap available = \emptyset$$

The final direct requirement is that a borrower may not have more than a predefined number of books checked out at one time. We introduce *maxbooks* to represent this predefined number, and state that the function which records the books borrowed by any specific user must have no more than *maxbooks* elements.

$$maxbooks : \mathbb{N}$$
$$\forall p : PERSON \cdot \#(checked\_out \triangleright \{p\}) \leq maxbooks$$

Having recorded the properties of the database which follow directly from the statement of the problem, we add an additional constraint: common sense tells us that books can only be checked out to people who are registered as staff or borrowers:

$$\text{ran } checked\_out \subseteq staff \cup borrowers$$

The transactions which are to be performed on the database impose some additional constraints on the state. Arising from transaction 5, there is a need to record which borrower last checked out a book:

$$last\_checked\_out : COPY \nrightarrow PERSON$$

We note that if somebody currently has a book checked out, then he must be the last person to have checked out that book!

$$checked\_out \subseteq last\_checked\_out$$

This is a state invariant and must be maintained by all transactions.

We need to record more information about each copy of a book in the library – its title, authors and subjects. To this end, we introduce the sets *TITLE*, *AUTHOR* and *SUBJECT* to represent book titles, author names and subject categories.

$$[TITLE, AUTHOR, SUBJECT]$$

The following schema defines what we need to know about each book:

```
┌─ BOOK ──────────────────────────
│ title : TITLE
│ authors : F AUTHOR
│ subjects : F SUBJECT
└─────────────────────────────────
```

Information about the copies in the library is then recorded in a mapping:

$$book\_info : COPY \nrightarrow BOOK$$
$$\text{dom } book\_info = stock$$

4.3.2 Abstract state specification

The requirements discussed above lead to the following description of the abstract state:

$$[PERSON, COPY, TITLE, AUTHOR, SUBJECT]$$
$$maxbooks : \mathbb{N}$$

BOOK
$$title : TITLE$$
$$authors : \mathbb{F} AUTHOR$$
$$subjects : \mathbb{F} SUBJECT$$

USERS
$$staff : \mathbb{P} PERSON$$
$$borrowers : \mathbb{P} PERSON$$

$$staff \cap borrowers = \varnothing$$

DB
$$stock : \mathbb{P} COPY$$
$$available : \mathbb{P} COPY$$
$$checked\_out : COPY \nrightarrow PERSON$$
$$last\_checked\_out : COPY \nrightarrow PERSON$$
$$book\_info : COPY \nrightarrow BOOK$$

$$(\text{dom } checked\_out) \cup available = stock$$
$$(\text{dom } checked\_out) \cap available = \varnothing$$
$$\forall p : PERSON \cdot \#(checked\_out \rhd \{p\}) \leq maxbooks$$
$$checked\_out \subseteq last\_checked\_out$$
$$\text{dom } book\_info = stock$$

LIB
USERS
DB

$$\text{ran } checked\_out \subseteq staff \cup borrowers$$

4.3.3 Initial abstract state

The system will be initialised with at least one member of staff. Since the requirements do not include any mechanism for altering either the staff or the borrowers, we assume that these sets will be provided as part of the initialisation. In order to allow for future development of these 'user-control' operations, our initialisation simply requires that there be at least one member of staff, since we assume that these operations will be restricted to staff members. When the system starts up, there are no books in the library, and there is no recorded history of any loans having taken place in the past.

$$Init\_USERS \triangleq [\ USERS' \mid staff' \neq \varnothing]$$

$$Init\_DB \triangleq [\ DB' \mid stock' = \varnothing \wedge last\_checked\_out' = \varnothing]$$

Now we have:

$$Init\_LIB \triangleq LIB' \wedge Init\_USERS \wedge Init\_DB$$

The 'Initialisation' theorem, which guarantees that an initial state exists, holds:

$$PERSON \neq \varnothing \vdash \exists \, LIB' \bullet Init\_LIB$$

4.3.4 Transaction specification

In order to specify the transactions available in our library system, we need a schema which introduces the 'before' and 'after' values:

$$\Delta LIB \triangleq LIB \wedge LIB'$$

We can divide the transactions into two broad categories: those which may only be performed by members of staff and those which can be performed by any registered user.

4.3.4.1 Staff transactions

Let us consider first the properties common to all the staff transactions: they involve the input of a name, which must be that of a member of staff, and they do not affect the users of the system.

```
┌─ Staff_trans ────────────────────────────────────
│ ΔLIB
│ id? : PERSON
├──────────────────────────────────────────────────
│ id? ∈ staff
│ θUSERS = θUSERS'
└──────────────────────────────────────────────────
```

The staff transactions may be further subdivided into three groups:

(1) counter transactions
(2) stock transactions
(3) staff enquiries.

(1) **Counter transactions**   The first group contains those transactions which might be carried out by a member of staff at the library counter. This group contains the *Check_out* and *Return* operations from requirement (1). Both of these involve a book and neither changes the stock of the library.

$$
\begin{array}{|l}
\hline
\quad Counter\_trans \underline{\hspace{6cm}} \\
\hline
Staff\_trans \\
copy? : COPY \\
\hline
copy? \in stock \\
stock' = stock \\
book\_info' = book\_info \\
\hline
\end{array}
$$

The check-out operation involves a book which must be available for loan. The record of checked-out books is updated and the new borrower is recorded as the last person to check out the book.

$$
\begin{array}{|l}
\hline
\quad Check\_out \underline{\hspace{6cm}} \\
\hline
Counter\_trans \\
borrower? : PERSON \\
\hline
copy? \in available \\
borrower? \in staff \cup borrowers \\
\#(checked\_out \rhd \{borrower?\}) < maxbooks \\
available' = available \setminus \{copy?\} \\
checked\_out' = checked\_out \cup \{copy? \mapsto borrower?\} \\
last\_checked\_out' = last\_checked\_out \oplus \{copy? \mapsto borrower?\} \\
\hline
\end{array}
$$

A book which is to be returned to the library must have been checked-out. It is recorded as being available for loan once more, and the record of the loan is removed. The record of who last checked out the book is not affected. Note that a *PERSON* is not required as input: we do not insist that a book should be returned by the same person who borrowed it, nor do we even check that the returner is known to the library.

```
┌─ Return ────────────────────────────────────────────────
│ Counter_trans
├──────────────────────────────────────────────────────────
│ copy? ∈ dom  checked_out
│ available' = available ∪ {copy?}
│ checked_out' = {copy?} ◁ checked_out
│ last_checked_out' = last_checked_out
└──────────────────────────────────────────────────────────
```

(2) Stock transactions   Staff transactions from the second group are concerned with altering the stock of the library. This group contains the *Add* and *Remove* operations from requirement (2). Both of these involve a book and neither alters the records of current loans.

```
┌─ Stock_trans ───────────────────────────────────────────
│ Staff_trans
│ copy? : COPY
├──────────────────────────────────────────────────────────
│ checked_out' = checked_out
└──────────────────────────────────────────────────────────
```

The copy identifier which is used for a new addition to the library must not already be in use. The copy is added to the stock and recorded immediately as being available for loan.

```
┌─ Add ───────────────────────────────────────────────────
│ Stock_trans
│ title? : TITLE
│ authors? : F AUTHOR
│ subjects? : F SUBJECT
├──────────────────────────────────────────────────────────
│ copy? ∉ stock
│ stock' = stock ∪ {copy?}
│ available' = available ∪ {copy?}
│ last_checked_out' = last_checked_out
│ book_info' = book_info ⊕ {copy? ↦ B}
│     where B : BOOK | B.title = title?
│                       B.authors = authors?
│                       B.subjects = subjects?
└──────────────────────────────────────────────────────────
```

When we remove a copy of a book from the library, we stipulate that the book must be available for loan: if it were not, we might well have a borrower who would be rather unhappy when the book was summarily removed from his grasp! We have decided not to keep any record of who last checked out a book which has been removed from the library.

Remove _____

Stock_trans
_____

$copy? \in available$
$stock' = stock \setminus \{copy?\}$
$available' = available \setminus \{copy?\}$
$last\_checked\_out' = \{copy?\} \lhd last\_checked\_out$
$book\_info' = \{copy?\} \lhd book\_info$

---

(3) **Staff enquiries**   The final group of staff transactions arises from requirements (4) and (5), and deals with enquiries which members of staff may need to answer. These transactions do not alter the database. Members of staff may wish to know what books have currently been borrowed by a particular user (requirement (4)). Note the output from this transaction consists of a set of copy identifiers together with all the information about each copy.

Borrowed_list _____

Staff_trans
$borrower? : PERSON$
$list! : \mathsf{F}(COPY \times BOOK)$
_____

$borrower? \in staff \cup borrowers$
$list! = \{c : COPY \mid$
$\qquad\qquad checked\_out(c) = borrower? \bullet (c, book\_info(c))\}$
$\theta DB = \theta DB'$

A member of staff can also ask who was the last borrower to check out a particular copy of a book (requirement (5)).

Last_borrower _____

Staff_trans
$copy? : COPY$
$borrower! : PERSON$
_____

$borrower! = last\_checked\_out(copy?)$
$\theta DB = \theta DB'$

4.3.4.2   User transactions
The second broad category of transactions contains those which can be performed by any registered user. These are enquiry operations and they

alter neither the users of the library nor the database itself. (We assume that the transactions of requirement (3) are restricted to registered borrowers and staff members, rather than being available to any member of the public, although this is not explicitly stated in the problem.)

```
┌─ User_trans ─────────────────────────────────
│ ΔLIB
│ id? : PERSON
│ ─────────────────────────────────────────────
│ id? ∈ staff ∪ borrowers
│ θLIB = θLIB'
```

We interpret transaction (3) of the informal requirements to mean: 'Get the list of books whose authors or subjects match a given description'. We therefore need 'matching' relations: each description is related to those authors and subjects which match it in some way.

[DESC]

```
│ A_match : DESC ↔ AUTHOR
│ S_match : DESC ↔ SUBJECT
```

A borrower may enquire about books by a particular author.

```
┌─ Author_enquiry ─────────────────────────────
│ User_trans
│ d? : DESC
│ list! : P BOOK
│ ─────────────────────────────────────────────
│ list! = {b : BOOK | b ∈ ran book_info ∧
│                 (b.authors ∩ A_match(|d?|) ≠ ∅)}
```

Similarly, a borrower may be interested in books on a particular subject.

```
┌─ Subject_enquiry ────────────────────────────
│ User_trans
│ d? : DESC
│ list! : P BOOK
│ ─────────────────────────────────────────────
│ list! = {b : BOOK | b ∈ ran book_info ∧
│                 (b.subjects ∩ S_match(|d?|) ≠ ∅)}
```

The third enquiry transaction covers the remaining half of requirement (4). An ordinary borrower may ask which books he has currently borrowed.

$$
\begin{array}{|l}
\hline
\_\,Self\_borrowed\_list \rule{6cm}{0.4pt} \\[4pt]
\quad User\_trans \\
\quad list! : \mathbb{P}\,BOOK \\[4pt]
\hline
\quad list! = \{c : COPY \,|\, checked\_out(c) = id? \bullet book\_info(c)\} \\
\hline
\end{array}
$$

4.3.4.3 Summary of transaction structure

The structure of the various available transactions is summarised in Fig. 4.1.

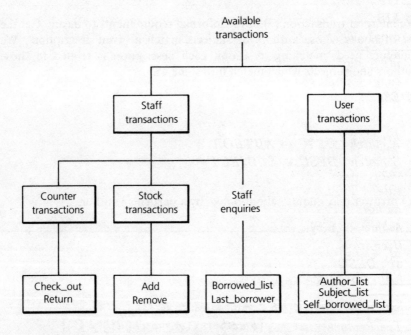

Fig. 4.1

4.3.5 Precondition investigation

In the previous section, we only described the successful behaviour of the transactions. We shall now summarise the conditions on inputs and starting states of the transactions described above. We will call these conditions the *preconditions* of the transactions. We will then give a first refinement, which will extend the descriptions of the transactions to cover behaviour when the conditions for successful behaviour are not met.

The precondition schemas are obtained by simply inspecting the schemas which describe the successful behaviours, and extracting the conditions on inputs and starting states. The precondition schemas are:

__ *Pre_Check_out* _____
LIB; $id?$, $borrower?$: $PERSON$
$copy?$: $COPY$

$id? \in staff$
$borrower? \in staff \cup borrowers$
$copy? \in available$
$\#(checked\_out \rhd \{borrower?\}) < maxbooks$

__ *Pre_Return* _____
LIB; $id?$: $PERSON$
$copy?$: $COPY$

$id? \in staff$
$copy? \in \mathrm{dom}\ checked\_out$

__ *Pre_Add* _____
LIB; $id?$: $PERSON$
$copy?$: $COPY$
$title?$: $TITLE$
$authors?$: $\mathbb{F}\ AUTHOR$
$subjects?$: $\mathbb{F}\ SUBJECT$

$id? \in staff$
$copy? \notin stock$

__ *Pre_Remove* _____
LIB; $id?$: $PERSON$
$copy?$: $COPY$

$id? \in staff$
$copy? \in available$

__ *Pre_Borrowed_list* _____
LIB; $id?$, $borrower?$: $PERSON$

$id? \in staff$
$borrower? \in staff \cup borrowers$

```
┌─ Pre_Last_borrower ──────────────────────────────
│ LIB; id? : PERSON
│ copy? : COPY
├──────────────────────────────────────────────────
│ id? ∈ staff
│ copy? ∈ dom last_checked_out
└──────────────────────────────────────────────────
```

```
┌─ Pre_Author_enquiry ─────────────────────────────
│ LIB; id? : PERSON
│ d? : DESC
├──────────────────────────────────────────────────
│ id? ∈ staff ∪ borrowers
└──────────────────────────────────────────────────
```

```
┌─ Pre_Subject_enquiry ────────────────────────────
│ LIB; id? : PERSON
│ d? : DESC
├──────────────────────────────────────────────────
│ id? ∈ staff ∪ borrowers
└──────────────────────────────────────────────────
```

```
┌─ Pre_Self_borrowed_list ─────────────────────────
│ LIB; id? : PERSON
├──────────────────────────────────────────────────
│ id? ∈ staff ∪ borrowers
└──────────────────────────────────────────────────
```

However, the stated conditions might not be sufficient to ensure successful behaviour, either because we have omitted some condition or because there is a precondition 'hidden' in one of the postcondition predicates. We guarantee that successful behaviour can be achieved under these stated conditions by proving the 'precondition theorems'.

$$Pre\_Check\_out \quad \vdash \quad \exists\, LIB' \bullet Check\_out$$
$$Pre\_Return \quad\quad \vdash \quad \exists\, LIB' \bullet Return$$
$$etc$$

An alternative to the approach outlined above would be to calculate the preconditions directly from the descriptions of the transactions. The 'precondition theorems' would then hold automatically.

4.3.6 Error actions

If an error condition is detected, we require that the state variables should remain unchanged and a report should be output.

```
┌─ Error ─────────────────────────────────────────────────
│ ΔLIB
│ r! : REPORT
├─────────────────────────────────────────────────────────
│ θLIB = θLIB′
└─────────────────────────────────────────────────────────
```

$$REPORT ::= \text{``unknown librarian''} \mid \text{``unknown borrower''}$$
$$\mid \text{``too many books''} \mid \text{``book not in stock''}$$
$$\mid \text{``book not available''} \mid \text{``book not checked out''}$$
$$\mid \text{``book in stock''} \mid \text{``book never out''}$$
$$\mid \text{``unknown user''} \mid \text{``OK''}$$

The following schema describes an unauthorised attempt to perform an operation which is restricted to members of staff.

```
┌─ Unknown_librarian ─────────────────────────────────────
│ Error
│ id? : PERSON
├─────────────────────────────────────────────────────────
│ id? ∉ staff
│ r! = "unknown librarian"
└─────────────────────────────────────────────────────────
```

The following schema describes an attempt to perform an operation which involves a borrower who is not known to the system.

```
┌─ Unknown_borrower ──────────────────────────────────────
│ Error
│ borrower? : PERSON
├─────────────────────────────────────────────────────────
│ borrower? ∉ staff ∪ borrowers
│ r! = "unknown borrower"
└─────────────────────────────────────────────────────────
```

The error which occurs when a borrower tries to borrow more than the predefined number of books that he is allowed is described by:

```
┌─ Too_many_books ────────────────────────────────────────
│ Error
│ borrower? : PERSON
├─────────────────────────────────────────────────────────
│ #(checked_out ▷ {borrower?}) ≥ maxbooks
│ r! = "too many books"
└─────────────────────────────────────────────────────────
```

The remaining errors all concern problems with a book, as summarised in the following schema.

$$BError \;\hat{=}\; [\; Error;\; copy? : COPY\,]$$

Some operations require the book to be in the stock of the library and available for loan, which gives us the following error schema.

```
┌─ Book_not_available ────────────────────────────────
│ BError
├──────────────────────────────────────────────────
│ (copy? ∉ stock  ∧  r! = "book not in stock")
│ ∨
│ (copy? ∈ stock\available  ∧  r! = "book not available")
```

We also need to know when the book has not already been checked out.

```
┌─ Book_not_checked_out ──────────────────────────────
│ BError
├──────────────────────────────────────────────────
│ (copy? ∉ stock  ∧  r! = "book not in stock")
│ ∨
│ (copy? ∈ available  ∧  r! = "book not checked out")
```

Other operations require that the book should not be in stock.

$$Book\_in\_stock \;\hat{=}\;$$
$$[\; BError \mid copy? \in stock \;\land\; r! = \text{``book in stock''}\,]$$

If a book has never been borrowed, we cannot ask who was the last person to borrow it.

```
┌─ Book_never_out ────────────────────────────────────
│ BError
├──────────────────────────────────────────────────
│ (copy? ∉ stock  ∧  r! = "book not in stock")
│ ∨
│ (copy? ∈ stock\ dom last_checked_out  ∧ r! = "book never out")
```

The following schema reports an attempt to perform a 'public' operation by someone who is not known to the system.

```
┌─ Unknown_user ─────────────────────────────────────────
│ Error
│ id? : PERSON
├───────────────────────────────────────────────────────
│ id? ∉ staff ∪ borrowers
│ r! = "unknown user"
└───────────────────────────────────────────────────────
```

We also need to give a report for operations which have been performed successfully.

$$Success \triangleq [\ r! : REPORT\ |\ r! = \text{``OK''}\ ]$$

We can now give descriptions of the total operations. Note that the cases which the error schemas have to cover are obtained by negating each of the predicates of the precondition schema in turn. So, for the *Check_out* operation, *Unknown_librarian* covers the case where the precondition *id?* ∈ *staff* is not met, *Unknown_borrower* covers the case where *borrower?* ∈ *staff* ∪ *borrowers* is not met etc. Our complete descriptions are given by the following equations.

$$
\begin{aligned}
T\_Check\_out \quad &\triangleq \quad (Check\_out \wedge Success) \\
&\quad \vee\ Unknown\_librarian \\
&\quad \vee\ Unknown\_borrower \\
&\quad \vee\ Book\_not\_available \\
&\quad \vee\ Too\_many\_books
\end{aligned}
$$

$$
\begin{aligned}
T\_Return \quad &\triangleq \quad (Return \wedge Success) \\
&\quad \vee\ Unknown\_librarian \\
&\quad \vee\ Book\_not\_checked\_out
\end{aligned}
$$

$$
\begin{aligned}
T\_Add \quad &\triangleq \quad (Add \wedge Success) \\
&\quad \vee\ Unknown\_librarian \\
&\quad \vee\ Book\_in\_stock
\end{aligned}
$$

$$
\begin{aligned}
T\_Remove \quad &\triangleq \quad (Remove \wedge Success) \\
&\quad \vee\ Unknown\_librarian \\
&\quad \vee\ Book\_not\_available
\end{aligned}
$$

$$
\begin{aligned}
T\_Borrowed\_list \quad &\triangleq \quad (Borrowed\_list \wedge Success) \\
&\quad \vee\ Unknown\_librarian \\
&\quad \vee\ Unknown\_borrower
\end{aligned}
$$

$$T\_Last\_borrower \quad\triangleq\quad (Last\_borrower \wedge Success)$$
$$\vee\ Unknown\_librarian$$
$$\vee\ Book\_never\_out$$

$$T\_Author\_enquiry \quad\triangleq\quad (Author\_enquiry \wedge Success)$$
$$\vee\ Unknown\_user$$

$$T\_Subject\_enquiry \quad\triangleq\quad (Subject\_enquiry \wedge Success)$$
$$\vee\ Unknown\_user$$

$$T\_Self\_borrowed\_list \quad\triangleq\quad (Self\_borrowed\_list \wedge Success)$$
$$\vee\ Unknown\_user$$

To verify that the operations described above do actually apply to all possible input situations, we need to check that the disjuncts partition the state. This follows trivially from the method used to describe the error schemas. Formally the check can be carried out by proving the 'implementability' theorems. For example, the theorem to be proved for the *Check_out* operation is

$$LIB;\ id?,borrower?:PERSON;\ copy?:COPY$$
$$\vdash$$
$$\exists\ LIB';\ r!:REPORT \bullet T\_Check\_out$$

4.4   DESIGN ANALYSIS

When we are writing a specification of a system, our aim is clear: we want to understand (and to explain to others) *what* the system is to do. Our choice of the components for the abstract state must reflect this aim. However, this abstract description of the state, and the operations on it, is not the best description for explaining *how* the system is to achieve its intended results. We need to describe the system at a different level of abstraction: the components of our design state will be very closely related to the data structures of the implementation, and the operations, at this level, will show how those components should change. Clearly we need to be precise about the relationship between these two views of our system, and we need to prove that the operations on the design state do in fact 'correspond' to the operations on the abstract state. We shall first describe the components of our design state and the predicates which are invariantly true about them. When we have recorded the connection between the abstract state and the design state, we will be able to prove that the initial design state 'corresponds' to an initial abstract state. We will give a specification for the design of the

Check_out transaction; the design versions of the other transactions can be obtained simply by following the guidelines given.

4.4.1 Design state signature

Our first decision is to have two collections of records. The first collection will have one record for each known *PERSON* and will contain all the information that we need to associate with a *PERSON*. The second collection of records is designed to contain information about copies of books – there will be one record for each known *COPY*.

Looking at the abstract state specification, we can see that we need the following information about each *PERSON*:

$$pid : PERSON$$
$$type : staff \mid borrower$$
$$borrowed : \mathsf{F}\ COPY$$
$$\# borrowed \leq maxbooks$$

borrowed records the books that are currently checked out by this *PERSON*. This information could just as easily be stored in the relevant *COPY* records by recording there the name of the borrower, but it is convenient also to have the information in the *PERSON* record: the *Borrowed_list* transaction needs to access this data by *PERSON*. When we look at the specification of the transactions which might affect this record (*Check_out* and *Return*), we see that the set *borrowed* will need to have insertions and deletions performed on it. We therefore envisage that it will be implemented as a doubly linked list.

The information that we need to record about each copy of a book is slightly more complex:

$$cid : COPY$$
$$status : in \mid out$$
$$borrower : person \langle\!\langle PERSON \rangle\!\rangle \mid none$$
$$details : BOOK$$

When a copy is first added to the library, the borrower field is set to *none*. However, from the time when it is first checked out, the borrower field always contains a *PERSON*, although the significance of this *PERSON* depends on the status field: if the book is 'in' the library, then the borrower field denotes the last person to check out the book (or *none* if the book has never been borrowed). If the book is 'out' of the library, then the borrower field denotes the current borrower (who must also be the last checker-out). The following state invariant must be maintained:

$$borrower = none \Rightarrow status = in$$

The *BOOK* schema contains two fields involving finite sets (*authors* and *subjects*). Since these fields will need to be searched but no insertions have to be carried out, these will be implemented as singly linked lists.

We have now progressed as far as we can by simply looking at the abstract state specification. We therefore move on to look at the specifications of the various transactions. Immediately we can see that several of them are going to require us to access a particular *PERSON* or *COPY* record. It would probably be very inefficient (given the likely size of the database) to search through a sequential structure, so we choose to have a directory structure to record the *COPY* information. There are likely to be fewer borrowers involved, so we decide to accept any reasonable implementation of a collection of records for *PERSON*.

We can model these structures as follows. We need a set of tokens, a file for the collection of *PERSON* records and an index and file for the collection of *COPY* records (Fig. 4.2).

$[TKN]$

$P\_file : PERSON \rightarrowtail P\_RECORD$

$C\_index : COPY \rightarrowtail TKN$

$C\_file : TKN \rightarrowtail C\_RECORD$

where *P_RECORD* and *C_RECORD* are schemas representing the *PERSON* and *COPY* records respectively (see Section 4.4.3).

Now, given a particular *PERSON* or *COPY*, we can reasonably efficiently access the relevant record. However, further examination of the specification of the operations shows that we often need to check whether a particular *PERSON* is a member of staff (to check for authorisation to perform the operation). Having verified that the *PERSON* is a member of staff, we do not need to examine or update the rest of that particular *P_RECORD*. Our

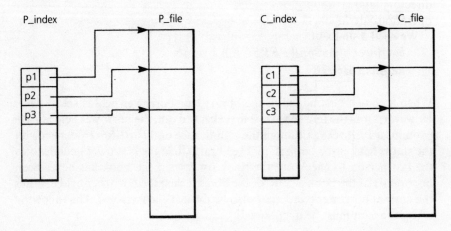

Fig. 4.2

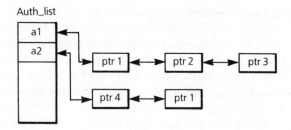

Fig. 4.3

present design would force us to retrieve the whole of the *P_RECORD* to check the status field. So instead we maintain an easily accessible list of staff members.

> *staff_list* : **F** *PERSON*

This will be implemented as a singly linked list: we only need to enquire whether an element appears in the list, not to update it.

The structures described so far are sufficient to enable us to implement, in a reasonably efficient manner, most of the required transactions. However, we come across a problem when we look at *Author_enquiry* and *Subject_enquiry*. In order to find all the books whose authors match a given string, we would have to search the whole of the *COPY* file to see which records matched. So instead we decide to build another index (Fig. 4.3).
We model this by

> *Auth_list* : *AUTHOR* ↔ *TKN*

where each author is related to some tokens, which are the keys to the *COPY* records of relevant books. We envisage the relation implemented as a directory and a doubly linked list – again, when the *Add* and *Remove* operations are invoked, we have to update the structure.

We need a similar structure for subjects (Fig. 4.4).

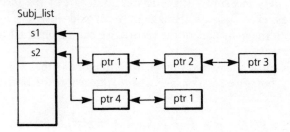

> *Subj_list* : *SUBJECT* ↔ *TKN*

Fig. 4.4

4.4.2 Design state invariants

Most of the invariants on the abstract state have been encoded in our design structures. However, these new data structures have introduced some invariants of their own. In each case where we have introduced redundant data, we must ensure that there is no inconsistency between the two versions of the data.

The first invariant that the new data structures introduce says that the directory structure must be consistent:

$$\text{ran } C\_index = \text{dom } C\_file$$

Now we move on to the consistency checks on redundant data. Clearly, *staff_list* must be consistent with *P_file*, i.e. the record corresponding to each element of *staff_list* must have its type field set to 'staff'.

$$staff\_list = \text{dom}(P\_file \rhd \{P\_RECORD | type = staff\})$$

Now we check that *Auth_list* and *Subj_list* are exactly consistent with the *authors* and *subjects* fields in the *COPY* records of the *COPY* file.

$$Auth\_list = (C\_file \; {}^\circ_\circ \; \lambda \, C\_RECORD \bullet details \; {}^\circ_\circ$$
$$\{b : BOOK; \, a : AUTHOR \mid a \in b.authors\})^{-1}$$
$$Subj\_list = (C\_file \; {}^\circ_\circ \; \lambda \, C\_RECORD \bullet details \; {}^\circ_\circ$$
$$\{b : BOOK; \, s : SUBJECT \mid s \in b.subjects\})^{-1}$$

Since *COPY* record and *PERSON* record both contain an *id*, we must be sure that, given an element of *COPY* or *PERSON*, the corresponding record in the main file should contain the same *id*.

$$\forall p : PERSON \mid p \in \text{dom } P\_file \bullet P\_file(p).pid = p$$
$$\forall c : COPY \mid c \in \text{dom } C\_index \bullet (C\_index {}^\circ_\circ C\_file)(c).cid = c$$

(Clearly, this *id* field is a redundant part of these two records, but it is useful as a safety measure – if the *id* were not part of the record, and the directory was ever lost or damaged, we would lose all of our data. However, with the *id* as part of the record, we can reconstruct the directory whenever we want.)

Finally, we must check that the record of the books that a particular user has currently borrowed is consistent with the record of borrowers in the *COPY* file.

$$\forall p : PERSON \mid p \in \text{dom } P\_file \bullet P\_file(p).borrowed =$$
$$\text{dom}(C\_index \; {}^\circ_\circ \; C\_file \rhd$$
$$\{C\_RECORD \mid status = out \wedge borrower = person(p)\})$$

4.4.3 Design state summary

$[TKN]$
$P\_TYPE ::= staff \mid borrower$
$C\_STATUS ::= in \mid out$
$C\_BORROWER ::= person \langle\!\langle PERSON \rangle\!\rangle \mid none$

$$
\begin{array}{|l}
\hline
\text{\_\_} P\_RECORD \text{_____} \\
\quad pid : PERSON \\
\quad status : P\_TYPE \\
\quad borrowed : \mathsf{F}\, TKN \\
\hline
\quad \# borrowed \leq maxbooks \\
\hline
\end{array}
$$

We have decided to record the books that a certain user has borrowed with a set of *tokens*, rather than *COPY* identifiers, since this is likely to make access to the *COPY* record more efficient.

$$
\begin{array}{|l}
\hline
\text{\_\_} C\_RECORD \text{_____} \\
\quad cid : COPY \\
\quad status : C\_STATUS \\
\quad borrower : C\_BORROWER \\
\quad details : BOOK \\
\hline
\quad borrower = none \Rightarrow status = in \\
\hline
\end{array}
$$

$$
\begin{array}{|l}
\hline
\text{\_\_} D\_USERS \text{_____} \\
\quad P\_file : PERSON \rightarrowtail\!\!\!\rightarrow P\_RECORD \\
\quad staff\_list : \mathsf{F}\, PERSON \\
\hline
\quad staff\_list = \mathrm{dom}(P\_file \rhd \{P\_RECORD \mid type = staff\}) \\
\quad \forall p : PERSON \mid p \in \mathrm{dom}\, P\_file \bullet P\_file(p).pid = p \\
\hline
\end{array}
$$

$$
\begin{array}{|l}
\hline
\_D\_DB \underline{\hspace{6cm}} \\
\hline
C\_index : COPY \rightarrowtail TKN \\
C\_file : TKN \rightarrowtail C\_RECORD \\
Auth\_list : AUTHOR \leftrightarrow TKN \\
Subj\_list : SUBJECT \leftrightarrow TKN \\
\hline
\operatorname{ran} C\_index = \operatorname{dom} C\_file \\
Auth\_list = (C\_file \,\S\, \lambda\, C\_RECORD \bullet details \,\S\, \\
\qquad \{b : BOOK;\, a : AUTHOR \mid a \in b.authors\})^{-1} \\
Subj\_list = (C\_file \,\S\, \lambda\, C\_RECORD \bullet details \,\S\, \\
\qquad \{b : BOOK;\, s : SUBJECT \mid s \in b.subjects\})^{-1} \\
\forall c : COPY \mid c \in \operatorname{dom} C\_index \bullet (C\_index \,\S\, C\_file)(c).cid = c \\
\hline
\end{array}
$$

$$
\begin{array}{|l}
\hline
\_D\_LIB \underline{\hspace{6cm}} \\
\hline
D\_USERS \\
D\_DB \\
\hline
\forall p : PERSON \mid p \in \operatorname{dom} P\_file \bullet P\_file(p).borrowed = \\
\quad \operatorname{dom}(C\_index \,\S\, C\_file \rhd \\
\qquad \{C\_RECORD \mid status = out \wedge borrower = person(p)\}) \\
\hline
\end{array}
$$

4.4.4 The Retrieve relation

We have recorded both the abstract and the design states individually, and we must now describe the mathematical connection between them. We record this relationship in the *Retrieve* schema, whose signature contains the abstract and design states, and whose predicate part shows how the components of the two states are related.

$$
\begin{array}{|l}
\hline
\_Retrieve \underline{\hspace{6cm}} \\
\hline
LIB \\
D\_LIB \\
\hline
staff = staff\_list \\
borrowers = (\operatorname{dom} P\_file) \setminus staff\_list \\
stock = \operatorname{dom} C\_index \\
available = \operatorname{dom}(C\_index \,\S\, C\_file \rhd \{C\_RECORD \mid status = in\}) \\
checked\_out = C\_index \,\S\, C\_file \,\S\, \\
\quad (\lambda\, C\_RECORD \mid status = out \bullet person^{-1}(borrower)) \\
last\,.checked\_out = C\_index \,\S\, C\_file \,\S\, \\
\quad (\lambda\, C\_RECORD \mid borrower \neq none \bullet person^{-1}(borrower)) \\
book\_info = C\_index \,\S\, C\_file \,\S\, (\lambda\, C\_RECORD \bullet details) \\
\hline
\end{array}
$$

We will need to use the *Retrieve* schema later to prove the correctness both of the initial design state and of the refinements of the transactions.

4.4.5 Initial design state

The recording of the initial design state is very similar to that of the initial abstract state:

```
┌─ Init_D_LIB ──────────────────────────────────
│  D_LIB'
│ ─────────────────────────────────────────────
│  staff_list' ≠ ∅
│  C_index' = ∅
│  Auth_list' = ∅
│  Subj_list' = ∅
└────────────────────────────────────────────────
```

We must be sure that the initial abstract and design states do in fact correspond according to the *Retrieve* relation. The theorem we have to prove is:

$$Init\_D\_LIB \vdash (\exists\, LIB' \bullet (Init\_LIB \wedge Retrieve'))$$

which is trivial to prove, because $PERSON \neq \varnothing$.

4.4.6 Transaction design methodology

For each operation we have specified, we want to reformulate the abstract specification in terms of the variables of the design state. We will follow the structure of the specification of the abstract operation in order to make the verification easier.

The design falls naturally into two main sections: we consider first the successful part of the operation, then the error cases.

4.4.6.1 *Design of the successful transaction*
We first describe, in terms of the variables of the design state, the conditions under which successful completion is required by the specification. Alternatively, the new preconditions for successful completion can be correctly derived from the abstract preconditions, by substituting expressions for variables, guided by equality predicates in *Retrieve*.

Next we describe the actual transformation required. This description is guided by the specification itself, the *Retrieve* relation and the intended operations on the data structures of the design state. Some properties can be derived from the specification by substituting expressions for variables as guided by the *Retrieve* relation. Often these properties need to be further constrained in order to prevent unintended freedom in the design. Other properties are formulated to suggest a particular operation on the data structure. Examples of each of these ways of obtaining the design transaction predicates are given below.

Finally, we have to verify our description against the specification. We have two checks to make. First we ensure that, when successful completion is expected, the design operation can actually complete, i.e. we need to prove:

$$PRE\_AOP\_ok \wedge R \vdash \exists\, CS' \bullet COP\_ok$$

where the *ok* suffix denotes a description of the successful completion. We also have to check that when the design operation has completed, it does indeed correspond to an acceptable successful transformation, i.e.:

$$COP\_ok \wedge R \vdash \exists\, AS' \bullet AOP\_ok \wedge R'$$

4.4.6.2   *Design of the error cases*

Having described the successful behaviour, we can now investigate the preconditions and describe the error cases. This is often very similar to the structure of the abstract operations, with particular error cases for the design operation corresponding to particular error cases for the abstract operation, except that the preconditions will now be described in terms of the concrete variables.

4.4.7   Design of the transactions

Just as for the abstract transaction, we need a schema describing the 'before' and 'after' states:

$$\Delta D\_LIB \triangleq D\_LIB \wedge D\_LIB'$$

Since we are following the structure of the abstract transactions, we have to describe staff transactions and counter transactions.

```
┌─ D_Staff_trans ──────────────────────────────────────
│ ΔD_LIB
│ id? : PERSON
├──────────────────────────────────────────────────────
│ id? ∈ staff_list
│ dom P_file' = dom P_file
└──────────────────────────────────────────────────────
```

Note that both of these predicates are direct consequences of the abstract operation *Staff_trans* and the predicate part of *Retrieve*: when we substitute the expressions for *staff* and *borrowers* given in *Retrieve* for the occurrences of these variables in the predicate part of *Staff_trans* (and do a little simplification), we get the two predicates given above in *D_Staff_trans*.

D_Counter_trans

D_Staff_trans
copy? : $COPY$

---

copy? $\in$ dom C_index
$C\_index' = C\_index$
$C\_file' \; \fatsemi \; (\lambda \, C\_RECORD \bullet details) =$
$\qquad C\_file \; \fatsemi \; (\lambda \, C\_RECORD \bullet details)$
$Auth\_list' = Auth\_list$
$Subj\_list' = Subj\_list$

The first, fourth and fifth predicates here are obtained directly from *Counter_trans* by substitution, while the third predicate is a slight simplification of what substitution would give. The second predicate is more interesting: straight substitution for *stock* (as guided by *Retrieve*) would only give us dom *C_index'* = dom *C_index*. This gives us the weakest refinement possible, but it allows the implementor the freedom to 'swap around' all the tokens, so long as, at the end of the operation, *C_index'* and *C_file'* are still consistent. We have made a design decision *not* to allow the implementor this freedom, so we insist that the whole of the function *C_index* remains unchanged by the *D_check_out* transaction.

D_Check_out _____

D_Counter_trans
borrower? : PERSON

$(C\_index \, \S \, C\_file)(copy?).status = in$
$borrower? \in \text{dom } P\_file$
$\#(P\_file(borrower?).borrowed) < maxbooks$
$C\_file' = C\_file \oplus \{CR, CR' : C\_RECORD \mid$
$\qquad\qquad \theta CR = (C\_index \, \S \, C\_file)(copy?)$
$\qquad\qquad cid' = cid$
$\qquad\qquad status' = out$
$\qquad\qquad borrower' = person(borrower?)$
$\qquad\qquad details' = details$
$\qquad\qquad \bullet \ C\_index(copy?) \mapsto \theta CR'\}$
$P\_file' = P\_file \oplus \{PR, PR' : P\_RECORD \mid$
$\qquad\qquad \theta PR = P\_file(borrower?)$
$\qquad\qquad pid' = pid$
$\qquad\qquad type' = type$
$\qquad\qquad borrowed' = borrowed \cup \{C\_index(copy?)\}$
$\qquad\qquad \bullet \ borrower? \mapsto \theta PR'\}$

The first predicate is obtained from *Check_out* by substituting for *available* as guided by *Retrieve*, and simplifying. The second predicate comes directly from *Check_out* by substitution. The precondition concerning the restriction on the number of books that a borrower may have out before a *Check_out* operation is expressed in terms of *P_file* rather than *C_file* because we expect that this is how the check will be implemented. The invariant on the design state (given in *D_LIB* above) guarantees that these two expressions for the precondition are equivalent. The *C_file* predicate is a major reformulation of the predicates about *available*, *checked_out* and *last_checked_out* obtained from *Check_out* by substitution. The version of the predicate which we give here is intended to give a hint to the implementor about the operation he might use on the eventual data type (i.e. that '*C_file* will remain unchanged except at one position, where the new value will be . . . '). The *P_file* predicate is a similar reformulation.

4.4.8 Precondition investigation

Once again, we have an obligation to investigate the conditions on inputs and starting states under which successful behaviour is expected.

Pre_D_Check_out _____

D_LIB
id?, borrower? : *PERSON*
copy? : *COPY*

---

id? $\in$ *staff_list*
copy? $\in$ dom *C_index*
$(C\_index \, {}_9^{\circ} C\_file)(copy?).status = in$
borrower? $\in$ dom *P_file*
$\#(P\_file(borrower?).borrowed) < maxbooks$

We have two proof obligations: we must prove that, if we are in a valid starting state for the abstract operation, then any corresponding design state must be a valid starting state for the design version of the operation. This is the 'Applicability' theorem.

$$Pre\_Check\_out \wedge Retrieve \vdash \exists\, D\_Lib' \bullet D\_Check\_out$$

The second proof obligation is to check that, if we are in a valid starting state, and we do actually perform the design operation, then we finish up in a valid design state, which corresponds, according to the *Retrieve* relation, to an abstract state that could have been reached by performing the abstract operation. This is the 'Correctness' theorem.

$$Pre\_Check\_out \wedge Retrieve \wedge D\_Check\_out$$
$$\vdash$$
$$\exists\, Lib' \bullet Check\_out \wedge Retrieve'$$

4.4.9 Error actions

Just as for the specification, we give descriptions of the error cases. The only difference is that the conditions are described in terms of the design state variables. For instance:

```
┌─ D_Error ──────────────────────────────────────
│ ΔD_LIB
│ r! : REPORT
├────────────────────────────────────────────────
│ θD_LIB' = θD_LIB
└────────────────────────────────────────────────
```

```
┌─ D_Unknown_librarian ──────────────────────────
│ D_Error
│ id? : PERSON
├────────────────────────────────────────────────
│ id? ∉ staff_list
│ r! = "unknown librarian"
└────────────────────────────────────────────────
```

We can now give a description of our total design operations.

$$
T\_D\_Check\_out \quad \triangleq \quad (D\_Check\_out \wedge Success)
$$
$$
\vee \ D\_Unknown\_librarian
$$
$$
\vee \ D\_Unknown\_borrower
$$
$$
\vee \ D\_Book\_not\_in\_stock
$$
$$
\vee \ D\_Book\_not\_available
$$
$$
\vee \ D\_Too\_many\_books
$$

Notice that we have decided to describe the two error cases that were previously described in *Book not available* in two schemas, *D_Book_not_available* and *D_Book_not_in_stock*. This is an almost entirely arbitrary decision, but it does make the algorithm description below slightly easier.

4.5   ALGORITHM DESIGN

We have now recorded the design of the operations in terms of the variables of the design state. We need to develop these operation designs further, towards our implementation language, so that the operations are described in terms of implementation language constructs (assignments, loops etc.) rather than predicates and set operations which are not directly implementable. We will describe the algorithm for the *Check_out* operation in Dijkstra's guarded command language [Dijkstra, 1975], with which we assume familiarity (a good introductory text is ([Gries, 1981]). During this algorithm design phase, we will also be developing and designing the interface we need to certain 'standard' abstract data types (linked lists, directories etc.). Although the guarded command language is not directly implementable, experience has shown that it is a fairly simple matter to translate an algorithm written in the guarded command language into a variety of procedural programming languages. We shall leave this final step to the interested reader, who is invited to translate the algorithm into his favourite programming language!

Our first observation is that the specification of *D_Check_out* is made up from several subspecifications (the successful case and each of the error cases). Each of these subspecifications is applicable only to certain inputs and starting states. We also notice that the error case specifications are much simpler than the successful case, so we decide to deal with them first. In particular, *D_Unknown_librarian*, *D_Unknown_borrower* and *D_Book_not_in_stock* have fairly simple preconditions, the truth of which can be established by single calls to functions on the standard abstract data types that we are assuming. For instance, the precondition for *D_Unknown_librarian* is *id?* $\in$ *staff_list*. From this we determine that the standard implementation for sets that we are using for *staff_list* must have a membership function, so we insert a call to the *member* procedure, with input parameters *staff_list* and *id?* and output *r*1. (*r*1 is a Boolean return code which will be set true if *id?* is found in *staff_list* and false otherwise.) We can similarly investigate the precondition for *D_Unknown_borrower*, and we see that we need a call to a procedure, in the interface to an implementation of a partial function, which determines whether a particular element is in the domain of the partial function. The investigation for *D_Book_not_in_stock* is slightly more interesting. The precondition is *copy?* $\in$ dom *C_index*, but, looking ahead, we can see that we will need the token which corresponds to *copy?*, both to check the precondition of *D_Book_not_available*, and, if necessary, to update the copy record. So we need a procedure for directories, *dirlookup*, which takes as input the name of a directory and an element, and produces as output both a return code and, if the element is found, the token which corresponds to that element. We therefore introduce a local variable *c_tkn* which will communicate the value of this token between parts of the implementation code.

So the first stage of algorithm design gives the following overall structure to the implementation.

T_D_Check_out

$\sqsubseteq$

```
r1, r2, r3 : Boolean;
c_tkn : TKN;
member(staff_list, id?, r1);
domlookup(P_file, borrower?, r2);
dirlookup(C_index, copy?, c_tkn, r3);
if  ¬r1           →    D_Unknown_librarian
▯   ¬r2           →    D_Unknown_borrower
```

$$\begin{array}{lll}
\| \quad \neg r3 & \rightarrow & D\_Book\_not\_in\_stock \\
\| \quad r1 \land r2 \land r3 & \rightarrow & D\_Book\_not\_available \\
& & \quad \lor \; D\_Too\_many\_books \\
& & \quad \lor \; (D\_Check\_out \land Success)
\end{array}$$

fi

Now the three error cases can be refined to simple assignments, since we have already established that they will only be invoked when their preconditions are met.

$$\begin{array}{lcl}
D\_Unknown\_librarian & \sqsubseteq & r! := \text{``unknown librarian''} \\
D\_Unknown\_borrower & \sqsubseteq & r! := \text{``unknown borrower''} \\
D\_Book\_not\_in\_stock & \sqsubseteq & r! := \text{``book not in stock''}
\end{array}$$

The second stage of the algorithm design has to deal with the error cases when the book is not available and when the borrower has *maxbooks* already checked out, as well as the successful case. We know that control will only reach this second stage of the algorithm when the preconditions for the first three error cases are not met (i.e. $r1 \land r2 \land r3$ is true), and when the variable *c_tkn* contains the value of the token which points to the relevant *C_RECORD*. To check whether the precondition of *D_Book_not_available* is true (i.e. $(C\_index_9^0 \; C\_file) \; (copy?).status = out$) we need to retrieve the *C_RECORD* corresponding to *copy?*. We can achieve this by calling the procedure *filelookup* with inputs *C_file* and *c_tkn* and outputs *CR* (a variable to contain the record) and *r4* (a return code). We also need to retrieve the *P_RECORD* corresponding to *borrower?*, and we store that record in the variable *PR*. To check whether the precondition of *D_Too_many_books* is true (i.e. $\#\,(P\_file(borrower?).borrowed) = maxbooks$), we need a call to the procedure *lengthdll* which returns the length of a doubly linked list, since this is how we decided to implement the borrowed set for each *P_RECORD*.

So we have the following structure for the second stage of the implementation:

$$\begin{array}{l}
D\_Book\_not\_available \\
\lor \; D\_Too\_many\_books \\
\lor \; (D\_Check\_out \land Success)
\end{array}$$

$$\sqsubseteq$$

$$\begin{array}{l}
PR : P\_RECORD; \\
CR : C\_RECORD; \\
r4, r5 : Boolean; \\
filelookup(C\_file, c\_tkn, CR, r4); \\
pflookup(P\_file, borrower?, PR, r5); \\
lengthdll(PR.borrowed, l);
\end{array}$$

```
if   CR.status ≠ in   →   D_Book_not_available
▯    l ≥ maxbooks      →   D_Too_many_books
▯    CR.status = in    →   D_Check_out ∧ Success
     ∧ l < maxbooks
fi
```

Again the two error cases are very easy to implement.

$$D\_Book\_not\_available \quad \sqsubseteq \quad r! := \text{``}book\ not\ available\text{''}$$
$$D\_Too\_many\_books \quad \sqsubseteq \quad r! := \text{``}too\ many\ books\text{''}$$

To complete the implementation, we need to give the code which refines $D\_Check\_out \land Success$. We know that the variables PR and CR contain the records corresponding to *borrower?* and *copy?*. We must first add the token corresponding to *copy?* to the list of books recorded as borrowed by *borrower?*, then we must update the partial function P_file at that one point. We achieve this with two calls to functions on the standard interfaces:

$$adddll(PR.borrowed, c\_tkn);$$
$$pfinsert(P\_file, borrower?, PR)$$

We must also update the status and borrower fields of the C_RECORD which corresponds to *borrower?*, and then update the file:

$$CR.status := out;$$
$$CR.borrower := borrower?;$$
$$fileinsert(C\_file, c\_tkn, CR)$$

Finally we must set the report value:

$$r! := \text{``}ok\text{''}$$

So the complete algorithm is as follows:

$$T\_D\_Check\_out$$

$$\sqsubseteq$$

$$r1, r2, r3 : Boolean;$$
$$c\_tkn : TKN;$$
$$member(staff\_list, id?, r1);$$
$$domlookup(P\_file, borrower?, r2);$$
$$dirlookup(C\_index, copy?, c\_tkn, r3);$$
```
if   ¬r1              →   r! := "unknown librarian"
```

⟦   ¬r2   →   r! := "*unknown borrower*"
⟦   ¬r3   →   r! := "*book not in stock*"
⟦   r1 ∧ r2 ∧ r3   →
   PR : *P_RECORD*;
   CR : *C_RECORD*;
   r4, r5 : *Boolean*;
   filelookup(*C_file*, *c_tkn*, *CR*, r4);
   pflookup(*P_file*, *borrower?*, *PR*, r5);
   lengthdll(*PR.borrowed*, l);
   if   *CR.status* ≠ *in*   →   r! := "*book not available*"
   ⟦   l ≥ *maxbooks*   →   r! := "*too many books*"
   ⟦   *CR.status* = *in*   →   *adddll*(*PR.borrowed*, *c_tkn*);
        ∧ l < *maxbooks*   *pfinsert*(*P_file*, *borrower?*, *PR*);
                                 CR.status := *out*;
                                 CR.borrower := *borrower?*;
                                 fileinsert(*C_file*, *c_tkn*, *CR*);
                                 r! := "*ok*"
   fi
fi

4.6   CONCLUSION

We have shown in this chapter that it is possible to progress from an abstract specification in Z, through a design, also in Z, to a collection of algorithms, recorded in Dijkstra's guarded command language. This work on refinement is important because it addresses one of the most serious problems that arises for users of formal methods: when a software engineer first learns about formal methods and wants to apply them, he inevitably uses them as early as possible in the software life cycle, i.e. in the specification phase. After a period of learning and familiarisation, it becomes very natural to use formal methods at the specification state, but the question inevitably arises, 'What can I do with these specifications?' We hope that we have shown one possible answer to this question: record a data refinement in Z, then develop an algorithm for each operation in the guarded command language. Work at IBM Hursley and in Oxford has shown that this is a viable approach to producing code from Z specifications.

However, more research is needed to discover whether this is the best 'refinement method'. This research probably needs to take the form of more case studies using the alternative methods. The approach we have concentrated our attention on has the advantage that it is meant to be a formalisation of the program development activities of experienced programmers: it is often the case that an experienced developer, having produced a Z specification of a system, will 'know' how to implement the specification. What we have attempted to do is to use this knowledge, but to record the steps more formally and give the option of proving each step correct with respect to its predecessors. More research is needed to produce proof rules which match the heuristics used by the experienced developer – these are likely to be applications of the existing proof rules to certain special cases to produce a simpler proof rule.

In conclusion, then, our case study has shown one of the possible routes from Z specification, through design, to code. We do not claim that ours is the best route – only further research can confirm or deny that claim – but at least it is a route that has been shown to be viable in an industrial environment.

4.7 ACKNOWLEDGEMENTS

The authors are grateful to Rachel Edge, Andy Gravell, Jim Woodcock and John Wordsworth for stimulating discussions and helpful suggestions.

4.8 REFERENCES

Bowen, J., Gimson, R. and Topp-Jorgensen, S. (1987) *The Specification of Network Services*, Technical Monograph PRG-61, Programming Research Group, University of Oxford.

Dijkstra, E. W. (1985) 'Guarded Commands, Nondeterminacy and Formal Derivation of Programs', *Communications of the ACM*, **18**(8), 453–7.

Gimson, R. (1987) *The Formal Documentation of a Block Storage Service*, Technical Monograph PRG-62, Programming Research Group, University of Oxford.

Gries, D. (1981) *The Science of Programming*, Springer-Verlag.

Hayes, I. J. (ed.) (1987) *Specification Case Studies*, Prentice-Hall International.

He, J., Hoare, C. A. R. and Sanders, J. W. (1987) 'Data Refinement Refined – Resumé', Programming Research Group, University of Oxford.

Hoare, C. A. R. and He, J. (1985) *The Weakest Prespecification*, Technical Monograph PRG-44, Programming Research Group, University of Oxford.

Jones, C. B. (1986) *Systematic Software Development using VDM*, Prentice-Hall International.

Kemmerer, R. A. (1985) 'Testing formal specifications to detect design errors', *IEEE Transactions on Software Engineering*, **SE11** (1), pp. 32–43.

King, S., Sorensen, I. H. and Woodcock, J. C. P. (1987) 'Z: Grammar and Concrete and Abstract Syntaxes. Version 1.1', Programming Research Group, University of Oxford.

Morgan, C. C. (1988) 'The Specification Statement', to appear in *ACM TOPLAS*.

Morris, J. (1987) 'A Theoretical Basis for Stepwise Refinement and the Programming Calculus', *Sci. Computer Programming*, **9**(3), 298–306.

Sanders, J. W. (1987) 'Refinement for Z', lecture notes, Programming Research Group, University of Oxford.

Spivey, J. M. (1987) 'The Z Notation – A Reference Manual', Programming Research Group, University of Oxford.

Spivey, J. M. (1988) *Understanding Z: A Specification Language and its Formal Semantics*, Cambridge University Press.

Wordsworth, J. B. (1987) *A Z Development Method*, IBM United Kingdom Laboratories Ltd.

Proceedings of the Fourth International Workshop on Software Specification and Design, April 3–4, 1987, Monterey, California, IEEE Computer Society Press.

4.9 SUMMARY OF PROOF OBLIGATIONS

4.9.1 Specification

Given a state S, and an intial state:

$$S\_init \triangleq [\ S' \mid init\_pred\ ]$$

we should prove the *Initialisation Theorem*:

$$\vdash \exists\, S' \bullet S\_init$$

For each operation, e.g.

$$F \triangleq [\ \Delta S;\, i?:X;\, o!:Y \mid f\_pred\ ]$$

with corresponding 'precondition':

$$Pre\_F \triangleq [\ S;\, i?:X \mid pre\_f\_pred\ ]$$

we should prove the *Precondition Theorem*:

$$Pre\_F \vdash \mathrm{pre}F$$

or

$$Pre\_F \vdash \exists\, S';\, o!:Y \bullet F$$

4.9.2 Design

Given a design state D, a retrieve relation R:

$$R \triangleq [\ S;\, D \mid retr\_pred\ ]$$

and an initial design state:

$$D\_init \triangleq [\ D'\ |\ D\_init\_pred\,]$$

we should prove the *Correctness of the initial design state*:

$$D\_init \vdash \exists\, S' \bullet (S\_init \wedge R')$$

For each design operation, e.g.:

$$D\_F \triangleq [\ \Delta D;\ i?:X;\ o!:Y\ |\ D\_f\_pred\,]$$

we should prove the *Applicability Theorem*:

$$Pre\_F \wedge R \vdash \exists\, D' \bullet D\_F$$

and the *Correctness Theorem*:

$$Pre\_F \wedge R \wedge D\_F \vdash \exists\, S' \bullet F \wedge R'$$

Chapter 5

Simple Transaction Processing and CSP

J. C. P. WOODCOCK

5.1 INTRODUCTION

In this chapter, an expanded version of [Woodcock, 1987], we show how the notations and theory of Communicating Sequential Processes may be used to model some simple aspects of transaction processing. We intend to show that the everyday concerns of concurrent software systems can be captured in a fairly natural way using CSP.

We describe below several primitives for transaction processing systems using Communicating Sequential Processes [Hoare, 1983; 1985]: the rather trivial case when there is just a single process in the system; multiple processes with simple locking protocol to achieve mutual exclusion; the same but with queuing for busy resources; and finally, discarding the locking of resources and instead taking the rather optimistic view that conflicts will probably not occur anyway. The study of these systems was inspired by the formal description and development of the lock manager in a major transaction processing system.

As we consider each system's requirements we capture them as individual predicates on the history of the system. The specifications that we give are of the *safety* properties of the system; implicitly we expect an implementation that is as live as possible. A *safety* specification says that the only things that can happen are specified; a *liveness* specification says that the safety properties do indeed happen. In the style that we are exploring in this chapter, the specifications often describe the *firing condition* for an event: if an event occurs, then some predicate must hold on the history of events up to that moment. Given our implicit requirement about liveness, we could have said that given that a firing condition holds, an event must not be refused.

The specification of each system is simply the conjunction of its requirements. This is indeed a powerful and natural way to capture the formal specification of a system. Less familiar, perhaps, is the approach to implementation in CSP process algebra. As the specification proceeds, we implement each requirement as a simple communicating process. Keeping both predicate and process as small as possible reduces the task of proving the implementation correct. In CSP, a parallel combination of processes corresponds to conjunction of their specifications; thus the implementation of the system is just the parallel composition of the processes implementing each requirement.

The result of the development process that we are describing is an implementation consisting of a highly distributed collection of synchronising and communicating processes. The laws of CSP are then used to transform the implementation. We could, if we wished, transform it into a form which is readily translated into occam [inmos, 1984] and run it on a collection of transputers, or transform it into an efficient, low-level systems program. Both of these transformations have been performed on the lock manager part of the system.

Section 5.5 contains an example of a formal proof of correctness of an implementation of part of a transaction processing primitive.

Section 5.9 contains a summary of the notation used in this chapter for the benefit of those unfamiliar with CSP.

5.2   A SINGLE PROCESS SYSTEM

We make a gross simplification – for the moment – that there is only one process in the system which accesses the data by reading and writing values. Let C be the set (type) of messages communicated between process and system.

In this system, if a and b are drawn from the set of values C, then the event *read.a* corresponds to the process reading the value a; *write.b* corresponds to the process writing the value b. Let:

```
R ≙ {read.c | c ∈ C}
W ≙ {write.c | c ∈ C}
```

It is not difficult to see that if there is just a single process, the data behaves as we would expect a programming variable would: if the process reads its contents, then it discovers the most recently written value. We can specify this: we want a process VAR with alphabet:

```
αVAR ≙ R ∪ W
```

and any trace tr of VAR must satisfy the following predicate (an even more concise specification follows from employing the CSP convention of using the name of a channel to denote the sequence of messages passed on that channel:

$$\forall c \in C \cdot \overline{tr}_0 = read.c \Rightarrow \overline{write}_0 = c \qquad):$$

```
VARSPEC ≙ (∀c ∈ C · tr̄₀ = read.c ⇒ tr⌈W₀ = write.c)
```

That is, if the last thing that happened in the system is that the process read a particular value c, then the most recently written value is also c. For this predicate to make sense, there must be at least one *write* before the first *read*. This specification is really describing the firing conditions for events in R. The events in W are left unconstrained.

An implementation is well-known (see [Hoare, 1985], p. 137):

$$
\begin{aligned}
\text{VAR} &\;\hat{=}\; (\text{write?x} \longrightarrow \text{VAR}_x) \\
\text{VAR}_x &\;\hat{=}\; (\text{read!x} \longrightarrow \text{VAR}_x \\
&\qquad |\text{write?y} \longrightarrow \text{VAR}_y)
\end{aligned}
$$

The process VAR is initially willing to participate only in a *write* event; having done so, it proceeds as VAR_x. In this behaviour, VAR is rather like a nice sort of uninitialised variable: it does not permit a *read* before the first *write*. VAR_x, on the other hand, behaves like a variable currently holding the value x. If the process tries to *read* the variable, it finds that it has the value x; this does not change the value (the variable continues to behave like VAR_x). However, the process can write a new value – say y – replacing the old one (the variable now behaves like VAR_y).

Note that we could have produced an implementation that avoids the use of a state variable, but it would have appeared rather more complicated.

We have adopted the convention that the specification for a process P is called $PSPEC$. In this chapter we have included only a few proofs; this is for reasons of space, rather than difficulty. In section 5.5 we present a formal proof that a process satisfies its specification. This proof together with several others taken from this chapter have been checked with a mechanical proof assistant. In a development of this kind, it is usual to do proofs in a routine manner: write down the predicate on traces and refusals; write down the behaviour in the process algebra; write down the proof of satisfaction. Developing all three together *does* offer valuable insights. The ability to use a machine to do much of the routine work seems to be an important factor in the feasibility of proving large systems correct.

5.3 MULTIPLE PROCESS SYSTEMS

5.3.1 A simple locking protocol

We now remove the restriction to a single process and specify a multiple tasking system. Let T be the set of task names; we shall use task names drawn from T to label events. For example, $t.lock$ will mean participation in the event *lock* by task t. We use the notation $t: P$ for the process P named by t; $t: P$ engages in the event $t.a$ whenever process P would have engaged in the event a. Furthermore, we use the notation $t.SPEC$ for the specification of process $t: P$, if process P satisfies the specification $SPEC$. Further descriptions may be found in sections 5.9 and 5.10.

The protocol we wish to describe involves tasks *locking* the data structure before accessing it. We add two new events to the interface: *lock* and *unlock*. Define:

$$
\begin{aligned}
\text{LOCKED} &\;\widehat{=}\; (\text{tr}{\downarrow}\text{lock} - \text{tr}{\downarrow}\text{unlock} = 1) \\
\overline{\text{LOCKED}} &\;\widehat{=}\; (\text{tr}{\downarrow}\text{lock} - \text{tr}{\downarrow}\text{unlock} = 0)
\end{aligned}
$$

LOCKED holds for the trace *tr* – which is free in the definition – just when there is one more *lock* in *tr* than *unlock*. Similarly, *UNLOCKED* holds just where there is an equal number of *lock* and *unlock* events in *tr*. A task may have either locked or not locked the data structure:

$$
\begin{aligned}
\alpha\text{LOCK} &\;\widehat{=}\; \{\text{lock}, \text{unlock}\} \\
\text{LOCKSPEC} &\;\widehat{=}\; (\text{LOCKED} \vee \overline{\text{LOCKED}})
\end{aligned}
$$

This is implemented by a process which simply alternates between *lock* and *unlock* events:

$$
\text{LOCK} \;\widehat{=}\; \mu X \cdot (\text{lock} \longrightarrow \text{unlock} \longrightarrow X)
$$

The definition of the process *LOCK* is recursive: it is the process *X* which first engages in the event *lock*, followed by *unlock*, and then it behaves like the process *X*.

Each task guarantees only to access information which it has previously locked. If a task *reads* a value from the data structure, the data structure must be locked:

$$
\begin{aligned}
\alpha\text{READ} &\;\widehat{=}\; R \cup \alpha\text{LOCK} \\
\text{READSPEC} &\;\widehat{=}\; (\overline{\text{tr}}_0 \in R \Rightarrow \text{LOCKED})
\end{aligned}
$$

Similarly, if a task *writes* a value from the data structure, the data structure must be locked:

$$
\begin{aligned}
\alpha\text{WRITE} &\;\widehat{=}\; W \cup \alpha\text{LOCK} \\
\text{WRITESPEC} &\;\widehat{=}\; (\overline{\text{tr}}_0 \in W \Rightarrow \text{LOCKED})
\end{aligned}
$$

These two requirements may be implemented by separate, but similar, processes: *READ* and *WRITE*. Instead, we offer their combination: the single process that permits reading and writing only after a *lock*, but before the next *unlock*. Let:

$$
\begin{aligned}
\alpha\text{READWRITE} &\;\widehat{=}\; \alpha\text{READ} \cup \alpha\text{WRITE} \\
&\;=\; \alpha\text{VAR} \cup \alpha\text{LOCK}
\end{aligned}
$$

$$
\text{READWRITE} \;\widehat{=}\; \mu X \cdot (\text{lock} \longrightarrow \mu Y \cdot (x : \alpha\text{VAR} \longrightarrow Y \\
\mid \text{unlock} \longrightarrow X))
$$

Notice that, because of the way in which we have chosen to implement *READWRITE*, with alternating *locks* and *unlocks*, it also satisfies *LOCK-SPEC*. Thus, when we put *LOCK* and *READWRITE* in parallel, we do not constrain the behaviour of *READWRITE* at all. Formally:

$$(\text{LOCK} \parallel \text{READWRITE}) = \text{READWRITE}$$

Each task must behave in the way that we have specified, and guarantee to follow the locking protocol:

$$\text{USESPEC} \triangleq (\forall t \in T \cdot t.\text{LOCKSPEC} \wedge t.\text{READSPEC} \wedge t.\text{WRITESPEC})$$

USESPEC is satisfied by:

$$\text{USE} \triangleq \parallel_{t \in T} t : \text{READWRITE}$$

Since conjunction in the specification corresponds to concurrency in the implementation, the universal quantification in *USESPEC* becomes parallel composition over a set in the process *USE*.

Each task relies on having *exclusive* access to locked information. So, when a task *t* acquires a lock, no other task may already have it:

$$\forall t, u \in T \cdot t.\text{LOCKED} \wedge u.\text{LOCKED} \Rightarrow t = u$$

MUTEXSPEC is implemented by a process that guarantees that a new lock cannot be acquired between a *lock/unlock* pair:

$$\text{MUTEX} = \mu X \cdot (\mathop{\square}_{t \in T} t.\text{lock} \longrightarrow t.\text{unlock} \longrightarrow X)$$

We can now combine *MUTEX* with what we already have:

$$
\begin{aligned}
\text{USE} \parallel \text{MUTEX} = \ &\mathop{\parallel}_{t \in T} \mu X \cdot (t.\text{lock} \longrightarrow \mu Y \cdot (x : \alpha(t : \text{VAR}) \longrightarrow Y \\
&\qquad\qquad\qquad\qquad\qquad\qquad\qquad |t.\text{unlock} \longrightarrow X)) \\
&\parallel \mu X \cdot (\mathop{\square}_{t \in T} t.\text{lock} \longrightarrow t.\text{unlock} \longrightarrow X) \\
= \ &\mu X \cdot (\mathop{\square}_{t \in T} t.\text{lock} \longrightarrow \mu Y \cdot (x : \alpha(t : \text{VAR}) \longrightarrow Y \\
&\qquad\qquad\qquad\qquad\qquad\qquad\quad |t.\text{unlock} \longrightarrow X))
\end{aligned}
$$

So far, all that we have done is to describe the interference that may be caused and that can be tolerated in the system. Now we must say how information changes or persists in the system. In fact, our multiple process system behaves not unlike a *single process* system: anyone reading the contents of a data structure discovers the most recently written value. Define a function which removes *any* task name from an event:

$$\texttt{tstrip} \triangleq \bigcup_{t \in T} \texttt{strip}_t$$

strip$_t$ is the function that removes the particular label t from an event [Hoare, 1983] (see also the Glossary of Symbols). *tstrip* then is the function that removes *any* label t from an event. Now, if we consider just the sequence of *reads* and *writes* and ignore which tasks initiated them, then our structure behaves just like a variable does. Since we do not care who initiates *read* or *write* events, we can use our forgetful function *tstrip* to disregard who does what:

$$\texttt{MVARSPEC} \triangleq \texttt{VARSPEC}[(\texttt{tstrip}^* \ \texttt{tr}) \upharpoonright \alpha\texttt{VAR} \ / \ \texttt{tr}]$$

tstrip*tr is the trace formed by applying *tstrip* to each element of *tr*. *VARSPEC* is a predicate on the free variable *tr*, and is in terms of the events in αVAR; therefore the definition of *MVARSPEC* which substitutes an expression for *tr*, ensures that expression mentions events only from αVAR.

Of course, we already know how to implement a variable, and we can reuse this implementation, with a suitable relabelling of event names. Since we are unconcerned with the identity of tasks, the inverse image under *tstrip* of *VAR* will give us a promiscuous version of *VAR*: it does not care who *reads* its values, or who *writes* new ones:

$$\texttt{MVAR} \triangleq \texttt{tstrip}^{-1} \ \texttt{VAR}$$

Expanding this we obtain:

$$\texttt{MVAR} = (\ \underset{t \in T}{\Box} \ \texttt{t.write?x} \longrightarrow \texttt{MVAR}_x)$$

where:

$$\texttt{MVAR}_x \triangleq (\ \underset{t \in T}{\Box} \ \texttt{t.read!x} \longrightarrow \texttt{MVAR}_x$$
$$| \ \underset{t \in T}{\Box} \ \texttt{t.write?y} \longrightarrow \texttt{MVAR}_y)$$

We have now completed our specification of a many process system. We have specified that tasks may *lock* the data structure, and that they may *read* and *write* only while they have the lock; we have specified that while a task has the lock it has exclusive access; and we have specified that the shared data behave like a variable. Our multiple process system must satisfy all three requirements:

$$\boxed{\text{MUSPEC} \triangleq (\text{USESPEC} \wedge \text{MUTEXSPEC} \wedge \text{MVARSPEC})}$$

Our system is implemented by:

$$\boxed{\text{MU} \triangleq (\text{USE} \parallel \text{MUTEX} \parallel \text{MVAR})}$$

We already have a simplified version of *USE* $\parallel$ *MUTEX*. Substituting this and our definition of *MVAR* into the definition of *MU* we obtain:

$$\boxed{\begin{aligned}
\text{MU} = \ &\mu X \cdot (\ \underset{t \in T}{\square} \ \text{t.lock} \longrightarrow \mu Y \cdot (x : \alpha(t : \text{VAR}) \longrightarrow Y \\
&\qquad\qquad\qquad\qquad\qquad\quad |\text{t.unlock} \longrightarrow X)) \\
&\parallel (\ \underset{t \in T}{\square} \ \text{t.write?x} \longrightarrow \text{MVAR}_x)
\end{aligned}}$$

where:

$$\boxed{\begin{aligned}
\text{MVAR}_x \triangleq \ &(\ \underset{t \in T}{\square} \ \text{t.read!x} \longrightarrow \text{MVAR}_x \\
&| \ \underset{t \in T}{\square} \ \text{t.write?y} \longrightarrow \text{MVAR}_y)
\end{aligned}}$$

Now, we can rewrite this to simplify it and eliminate the remaining concurrency symbol, obtaining:

$$\boxed{\begin{aligned}
\text{MU} = (\ &\underset{t \in T}{\square} \ \text{t.lock} \longrightarrow (\text{t.unlock} \longrightarrow \text{MU} \\
&\qquad\qquad\qquad\quad |\text{t.write?x} \longrightarrow \text{MU}_{t,x}))
\end{aligned}}$$

where:

$$\boxed{\begin{aligned}
\text{MU}_x \quad &\triangleq \ (\ \underset{t \in T}{\square} \ \text{t.lock} \longrightarrow \text{MU}_{t,x}) \\
\text{MU}_{t,x} &\triangleq \ (\text{t.unlock} \longrightarrow \text{MU}_x \\
&\qquad |\text{t.read!x} \longrightarrow \text{MU}_{t,x} \\
&\qquad |\text{t.write?y} \longrightarrow \text{MU}_{t,y})
\end{aligned}}$$

So *MU* is a process that allows an external choice as to which task gains the lock; only *that* task may *read* or *write* values to the data structure, until that same task yields the lock. It also ensures that a value is written to the data structure before a value can be read.

5.3.2 Queuing for busy resources

The system described in the last section suffers from the dangers of infinite overtaking: an unlucky task wanting a lock may *always* be unsuccessful and be continually pre-empted by faster tasks. We shall try to solve this by serving requests for locks in order. We introduce a new event: *request*. Let:

$$
\begin{aligned}
\text{REQ1} &\triangleq (\text{tr}{\downarrow}\text{request} - \text{tr}{\downarrow}\text{lock} = 1) \\
\overline{\text{REQ1}} &\triangleq (\text{tr}{\downarrow}\text{request} - \text{tr}{\downarrow}\text{lock} = 0) \\
\text{REQ2} &\triangleq (\text{tr}{\downarrow}\text{request} - \text{tr}{\downarrow}\text{unlock} = 1) \\
\overline{\text{REQ2}} &\triangleq (\text{tr}{\downarrow}\text{request} - \text{tr}{\downarrow}\text{unlock} = 0)
\end{aligned}
$$

Each task may have at most one outstanding request:

$$
\begin{aligned}
\alpha\text{REQUEST1} &\triangleq \{\text{request}, \text{lock}\} \\
\text{REQUEST1SPEC} &\triangleq (\text{REQ1} \lor \overline{\text{REQ1}}) \\
\alpha\text{REQUEST2} &\triangleq \{\text{request}, \text{unlock}\} \\
\text{REQUEST2SPEC} &\triangleq (\text{REQ2} \lor \overline{\text{REQ2}})
\end{aligned}
$$

These specifications should by now be quite familiar; they have the implementations:

$$
\begin{aligned}
\text{REQUEST1} &\triangleq \mu X \cdot (\text{request} \longrightarrow \text{lock} \longrightarrow X) \\
\text{REQUEST2} &\triangleq \mu X \cdot (\text{request} \longrightarrow \text{unlock} \longrightarrow X)
\end{aligned}
$$

We need to say how these *requests* get serviced. Define, for each task t and event e, a projection which tells us which task initiated an event:

$$
\text{task } t.e = t
$$

Also, define the sets of all $t.lock$ events and $t.request$ events, for all possible t:

$$
\begin{aligned}
\text{Tlock} &\triangleq \text{tstrip}^{-1} \text{ lock} \\
\text{Treq} &\triangleq \text{tstrip}^{-1} \text{ request}
\end{aligned}
$$

Our requirement is that a task obtaining a lock must be the next one deserving it: that is, the longest outstanding request should be served next:

$$
\text{QSPEC} \triangleq \text{task}^*(\text{tr} \upharpoonright \text{Tlock}) \leq \text{task}^*(\text{tr} \upharpoonright \text{Treq})
$$

The expression $tr \upharpoonright Tlock$ denotes the sequence of $t.lock$ events in the trace. $tr.task^* (tr \upharpoonright Tlock)$ is just the sequence of the names of those tasks which gained the lock. Similarly, $task^* (tr \upharpoonright Treq)$ is just the sequence of the names of those tasks which issued requests for the lock. *QSPEC* says that the sequence of names of tasks gaining the lock is a *prefix* of the sequence of names of tasks requesting the lock. It is reminiscent of the specification of a buffer: what comes out is a *prefix* of what goes in. This suggests an implementation which is similar to that of a buffer:

$$
\begin{aligned}
\text{Q} &\;\hat{=}\; \text{Q}_{\langle\rangle} \\
\text{Q}_{\langle\rangle} &\;\hat{=}\; (\;\underset{r\in T}{\square}\; \text{r.request} \longrightarrow \text{Q}_{\langle x\rangle}) \\
\text{Q}_{\langle t\rangle^\frown s} &\;\hat{=}\; (\text{t.lock} \longrightarrow \text{Q}_s \\
&\qquad |\;\underset{r\in T}{\square}\; \text{r.request} \longrightarrow \text{Q}_{\langle t\rangle^\frown s^\frown\langle x\rangle})
\end{aligned}
$$

Initially, the queue of requests is empty, and the process is willing to accept only a request. When there is at least one request, the task at the front of the queue may obtain the lock, or further requests may be added to the *end* of the queue. This is where the queuing discipline is encoded.

A 'fair' multiple process system behaves like our earlier multiple process system, allows at most one outstanding request per task, and has the queuing discipline that we have described:

$$
\begin{aligned}
\text{FAIRMUSPEC} \;\hat{=}\; (\;&\text{MUSPEC} \wedge \text{QSPEC} \wedge \\
&\forall t \in T \cdot t.\text{REQUEST1SPEC} \wedge t.\text{REQUEST2SPEC})
\end{aligned}
$$

$$
\text{FAIRMU} \;\hat{=}\; (\text{MU} \parallel \text{Q} \parallel \underset{t\in T}{\mid\mid} (t : \text{REQUEST1} \parallel t : \text{REQUEST2}))
$$

Of course, in this section we have only been fooling ourselves: we have pushed the problem back from getting the lock to requesting one. As before, a fast task might get into the queue, acquire the lock, release it, and get into the queue again before a slower one gets its act together. Thus it is slightly misleading – in fact downright lying – to call this solution 'fair'. As pointed out in [Hoare, 1985], the correct solution to this problem is probably to regard it as insoluble, because if any task is particularly determined on having so much access to a data structure, then someone – this task or another requiring access – will inevitably be disappointed. In CSP, we cannot distinguish between a task that takes an infinite amount of time to require access to a particular data structure, and one which does require access, but is being discriminated against by our transaction processing system. It seems that in our Kafkaesque world paranoia is indistuinguishable from genuine persecution. However, in practical terms, we have merely decided to delegate to the implementor the responsibility of ensuring that any desired event that is possible takes place within an acceptable period of time. So we ask that the implementation ensures that requests are serviced in an even-handed way. Fortunately, an implementation may find it a lot easier to be fair to requests than to locks, since the likelihood of a queue for requests may well be negligible. Of course, deadlock and unacceptable delay remain an unaddressed problem.

5.4   AN OPTIMISTIC APPROACH

The last section dealt with a system which allows multiple processes to gain mutually exclusive access to shared data by *locking*. It can handle contention for resources by allocating them on a first-come, first-served basis. In this section we consider a different strategy: each task rather optimistically assumes that there will be no interference from other tasks, and so may go blithely about its transaction. But there must always be a day of reckoning: upon completion of a transaction, the system examines whether, with hindsight, the case for optimism was justified or not. If indeed there has been no interference, then the transaction is committed; if interference was possible, then the offending transaction is deemed not to have occurred. Clearly, the suitability of this approach depends on the character of the individual application.

We introduce some new events: *start, comnull, comread, comwrite,* and *fail.* We shall have a different structure for our transactions than before. A transaction has a start point, and may be finalised in one of four ways: it might be the null transaction; it might be a read-only transaction; it might also have written to the data structure; or it might fail in some way. Which of the options are available to a transaction at any time will depend on the events comprising the transaction, and the interference that the transaction might cause, or might have to tolerate.

Our specification starts in a familiar way. Let:

$$
\begin{aligned}
\text{Commit} &\;\hat{=}\; \{\text{comnull, comread, comwrite}\} \\
\text{Final} &\;\hat{=}\; \text{Commit} \cup \{\text{fail}\}
\end{aligned}
$$

and define:

$$
\begin{aligned}
\text{ST} &\;\hat{=}\; (tr{\downarrow}start - tr{\upharpoonright}\text{Final} = 1) \\
\overline{\text{ST}} &\;\hat{=}\; (tr{\downarrow}start - tr{\upharpoonright}\text{Final} = 0)
\end{aligned}
$$

We shall require that transactions have unique names: a transaction will only be started *once*:

$$
\begin{aligned}
\alpha\text{UNIQUE} &\;\hat{=}\; \{\text{start}\} \\
\text{UNIQUESPEC} &\;\hat{=}\; (tr{\downarrow}start \leq 1)
\end{aligned}
$$

$$
\text{UNIQUE} \;\hat{=}\; (start \longrightarrow \text{STOP})
$$

Transactions start and then they are finalised either by being committed or by failing:

$$
\begin{aligned}
\alpha\text{TRANS} &\;\hat{=}\; \{\text{start}\} \cup \text{Final} \\
\text{TRANSSPEC} &\;\hat{=}\; (\text{ST} \vee \overline{\text{ST}})
\end{aligned}
$$

This specification is rather like *LOCKSPEC*; not surprisingly its implementation is similar to *LOCK*:

$$\text{TRANS} \triangleq \mu X \cdot (\text{start} \longrightarrow x : \text{Final} \longrightarrow X)$$

Reading and writing may only be done within transactions:

$$\alpha \text{RWTRANS} \quad \triangleq \quad \alpha \text{TRANS} \cup \alpha \text{VAR}$$
$$\text{RWTRANSSPEC} \triangleq \quad (\overline{\text{tr}_0} \in \alpha \text{VAR} \Rightarrow \text{ST})$$

This specification is again familiar: it is similar to both *READSPEC* and *WRITESPEC*. Its implementation is correspondingly straightforward:

$$\text{RWTRANS} \triangleq \mu X \cdot (\text{start} \longrightarrow \mu Y \cdot (x : \alpha \text{VAR} \longrightarrow Y$$
$$|\, x : \text{Final} \longrightarrow X))$$

A transaction must satisfy all three requirements: it may only be started once, and may only end by being committed or by failing, and reading and writing may only be carried out during transactions.

$$\text{TRANSACTSPEC} \triangleq (\text{UNIQUESPEC} \wedge \text{TRANSSPEC} \wedge \text{RWTRANSSPEC})$$

This is implemented as:

$$\text{TRANSACT} \triangleq (\text{UNIQUE} \parallel \text{TRANS} \parallel \text{RWTRANS})$$

Simplifying this, we obtain:

$$\text{TRANSACT} = (\text{start} \longrightarrow \mu X \cdot (x : \alpha \text{VAR} \longrightarrow X$$
$$|\, x : \text{Final} \longrightarrow \text{STOP}))$$

This shows quite clearly that a transaction can only occur once, is either committed or fails, and that reading and writing is only permitted during the transaction.

The three commit events for a particular transaction *t* are each labelled by *t* taken from *T*, which we now regard as the set of *transaction names*:

$$\text{Commit}_t \triangleq \text{strip}_t^{-1} \text{Commit}$$

Let *committed s* denote the set of names of *successfully completed* transactions in some trace *s*:

$$\text{committed } s \triangleq \{t \in T \mid s \restriction \text{Commit}_t \neq \langle \rangle\}$$

Of interest at the start of each transaction is the most recently committed value – if it exists. The sequence of *write* events made by successfully committed transactions in a trace *s* is:

$$\text{succwr } s \,\hat{=}\, s \upharpoonright \{\text{t.write.c} \mid \text{t} \in \text{committed } s \wedge c \in C\}$$

If this is not empty, then *lastwr s* is its last element, where:

$$\text{lastwr } s \,\hat{=}\, \overline{\text{succwr } s_0}$$

The view that each transaction has of the shared data structure simply consists of the *lastwritten* value – if it exists – followed by the *read*s and *write*s of the transaction itself. From each of these viewpoints the data structure appears as though it were a variable, possibly with an initial value. If we have:

$$W_t \,\hat{=}\, \text{strip}_t^{-1} \, W$$

then the requirement is:

$$
\begin{aligned}
\text{OVARSPEC} \;\hat{=}\; &\forall t \in T, c \in C \cdot \overline{\text{tr}}_0 = \text{t.read.c} \Rightarrow \\
&(\text{tr} \upharpoonright W_t = \langle\rangle \wedge \exists u \in T \cdot \text{lastwr tr} = \text{u.write.c}) \vee \\
&(\text{tr} \upharpoonright W_t \neq \langle\rangle \wedge \overline{\text{tr} \upharpoonright W_{t_0}} = \text{t.write.c})
\end{aligned}
$$

This should be reminiscent of the specification of a variable, but with a few extra bits and pieces. If a transaction *t* reads the value *c* from the data structure, then one of two cases must hold:

(1) Transaction *t* has not previously written a value: in which case *c* is equal to the last successfully committed written value.
(2) Transaction *t* has written a value: in which case the last value was also *c*.

This is implemented by a process that maintains a state containing the last successfully committed value, and the last written value for each transaction:

$$
\begin{aligned}
\text{OVAR} \quad &\hat{=}\quad \text{OVAR}(\bot, \{\}) \\
\text{OVAR}(v, f) \quad &\hat{=}\quad \Big(\underset{t \in T}{\Box} \; \text{t.start} \longrightarrow \text{OVAR}(v, f \oplus \{t \mapsto v\}) \\
&\qquad \mid \underset{t \in T \mid (f\,t) \neq \bot}{\Box} \text{t.read!}(f\,t) \longrightarrow \text{OVAR}(v, f) \\
&\qquad \mid \underset{t \in T}{\Box} \; \text{t.write?}x \longrightarrow \text{OVAR}(v, f \oplus \{t \mapsto x\}) \\
&\qquad \mid \underset{t \in T}{\Box} \; x : \text{Commit}_t \longrightarrow \text{OVAR}((f\,t), f)\Big)
\end{aligned}
$$

This *optimistic variable OVAR* initially behaves like $OVAR(\bot, \{\})$, for some distinguished value $\bot$. The second definition describes the behaviour of $OVAR(v, f)$ for some value of the shared data structure $v \in C$, and some function f: $T \rightarrow C$. When a transaction *t* starts, the function f is updated with the maplet $\{t \mapsto v\}$. Values may be read or written by transaction *t*; these are operations on *t*'s copy of the data structure in the mapping *f*. However, *OVAR* never engages in the event $t.read.\perp$, for any *t*. Finally, when transaction *t* is successfully committed, the shared value of the data structure is updated with the final value computed by *t*.

We can make the intuitive link between *OVAR* and *VAR* precise by being more explicit about the 'view' that each transaction has of the shared data structure. If:

$$
\begin{aligned}
\mathtt{initial_t} &\triangleq \begin{cases} \mathtt{lastwr\ (tr\ \underline{before}\ t.start)} & \text{if } \mathtt{succwr\ tr} \neq \langle\rangle \\ & \text{and } \mathtt{tr \upharpoonright W_t} = \langle\rangle \\ \langle\rangle & \text{otherwise} \end{cases} \\[6pt]
\mathtt{view_t} &\triangleq \mathtt{initial\,\hat{}\,(tr \upharpoonright \alpha(t:VAR))}
\end{aligned}
$$

then we can prove that:

$$
\mathtt{OVARSPEC} \Rightarrow \forall t \in T \cdot \mathtt{VARSPEC[tstrip^*\ view_t\ /\ tr]}
$$

That is, each view of the shared data structure reveals it to be just like a variable – no interference, no nasty surprises.

Now consider the various commit events. *comnull* corresponds to finalising the null transaction, so, if a transaction says that it made no access to a data structure, then this must be the case:

$$
\begin{aligned}
\alpha\mathtt{NULL} &\triangleq \{\mathtt{comnull}\} \cup \alpha\mathtt{VAR} \\
\mathtt{NULLSPEC} &\triangleq (\overline{\mathtt{tr}}_0 = \mathtt{comnull} \Rightarrow \mathtt{tr \upharpoonright \alpha VAR} = \langle\rangle)
\end{aligned}
$$

Reading or writing *disables* the *comnull* event:

$$
\begin{aligned}
\mathtt{NULL} \triangleq \mu X \cdot\ (&\mathtt{comnull} \longrightarrow X \\
&|\mathtt{x}: \alpha\mathtt{VAR} \longrightarrow \mathtt{STOP_{\{comnull\}}} \parallel \mathtt{RUN_{\alpha VAR}})
\end{aligned}
$$

A transaction finalised with a *comread* event must have read something:

$$
\begin{aligned}
\alpha\mathtt{CR1} &\triangleq \{\mathtt{comread}\} \cup R \\
\mathtt{CR1SPEC} &\triangleq (\overline{\mathtt{tr}}_0 = \mathtt{comread} \Rightarrow \mathtt{tr \upharpoonright R} \neq \langle\rangle)
\end{aligned}
$$

but not written anything:

$$
\begin{aligned}
\alpha\mathtt{CR2} &\triangleq \{\mathtt{comread}\} \cup W \\
\mathtt{CR2SPEC} &\triangleq (\overline{\mathtt{tr}}_0 = \mathtt{comread} \Rightarrow \mathtt{tr \upharpoonright W} = \langle\rangle)
\end{aligned}
$$

So reading *enables* the *comread* event:

$$
\mathtt{CR1} \triangleq (\mathtt{x}: R \longrightarrow \mathtt{RUN_{\{comread\} \cup R}})
$$

and writing *disables* it:

$$\text{CR2} \triangleq \mu X \cdot (\text{comread} \longrightarrow X$$
$$|x : W \longrightarrow \text{STOP}_{\{\text{comread}\}} \parallel \text{RUN}_W)$$

Putting these two together we get:

$$(\text{CR1} \parallel \text{CR2}) = (x : R \longrightarrow \mu X \cdot (x : R \longrightarrow X$$
$$|\text{comread} \longrightarrow X$$
$$|x : W \longrightarrow \text{RUN}_{\alpha\text{VAR}})$$
$$|x : W \longrightarrow \text{RUN}_{\alpha\text{VAR}})$$

If a transaction says that it has written to the data structure, then it must not be lying:

$$\alpha\text{CW1} \triangleq \{\text{comwrite}\} \cup W$$
$$\text{CW1SPEC} \triangleq (\overline{tr}_0 = \text{comwrite} \Rightarrow tr \upharpoonright W \neq \langle\rangle)$$

Writing *enables* the *comwrite* event:

$$\text{CW1} \triangleq (x : W \longrightarrow \text{RUN}_{\{\text{comwrite}\}\cup W})$$

Adding this to $(CR1 \parallel CR2)$ we obtain:

$$(\text{CR1} \parallel \text{CR2} \parallel \text{CW1}) = (x : R \longrightarrow \mu X \cdot (x : R \longrightarrow X$$
$$|\text{comread} \longrightarrow X$$
$$|x : W \longrightarrow \text{RUN}_{\{\text{comwrite}\}\cup\alpha\text{VAR}})$$
$$|x : W \longrightarrow \text{RUN}_{\{\text{comwrite}\}\cup\alpha\text{VAR}})$$

If we now add to this the process *NULL*, we get a description of how processes may be finalised:

$$\text{FINAL} \triangleq (\text{NULL} \parallel \text{CR1} \parallel \text{CR2} \parallel \text{CW1})$$
$$= \mu X \cdot (\text{comnull} \longrightarrow X$$
$$|x : R \longrightarrow \mu Y \cdot (x : R \longrightarrow Y$$
$$|\text{comread} \longrightarrow Y$$
$$|x : W \longrightarrow \text{RUN}_{\{\text{comwrite}\}\cup\alpha\text{VAR}})$$
$$|x : W \longrightarrow \text{RUN}_{\{\text{comwrite}\}\cup\alpha\text{VAR}})$$

A transaction t cannot be finalised with a $t.comread$ or $t.comwrite$ event if there has been an update of the data structure during t's lifetime. The simplest way of ensuring this is to say that no other transaction can have been finalised with a *comwrite* since t started. No interference has been caused to t by u if:

$$\alpha\text{NOINT}_{t,u} \triangleq \{t.\text{start}, t.\text{comread}, t.\text{comwrite}, u.\text{comwrite}\}$$
$$\text{NOINT}_{t,u}\text{SPEC} \triangleq (\overline{tr}_0 \in \{t.\text{comread}, t.\text{comwrite}\} \Rightarrow$$
$$\overline{tr}'_0 = t.\text{start})$$

This implementation of this requirement must ensure that *u.comwrite* disables *t.comread* and *t. comwrite* events:

$$
\begin{aligned}
&\text{NOINT}_{t,u} \triangleq \\
&\quad \mu X \cdot (\text{t.start} \longrightarrow \\
&\qquad\qquad (x : \{\text{t.comread}, \text{t.comwrite}\} \longrightarrow \text{u.comwrite} \longrightarrow \text{STOP} \\
&\qquad\qquad |\text{u.comwrite} \longrightarrow \text{STOP}) \\
&\qquad |\text{u.comwrite} \longrightarrow \text{t.start} \longrightarrow \\
&\qquad\qquad x : \{\text{t.comread}, \text{t.comwrite}\} \longrightarrow \text{STOP})
\end{aligned}
$$

We have now completed the description of the optimistic transaction processing primitives. Our full specification is:

$$
\begin{aligned}
\text{OPTSPEC} \triangleq (&\text{OVARSPEC}\wedge \\
&\forall t \in T \cdot \text{t.TRANSACTSPEC} \wedge \text{t.FINALSPEC}\wedge \\
&\quad \forall u \in T \cdot u \neq t \Rightarrow \text{NOINT}_{t,u}\text{SPEC})
\end{aligned}
$$

That is, the shared data behaves like an optimistic variable, reading and writing can only be done within transactions which have unique names, transactions must be finalised in the manner described, and the success of a transaction depends on the interference which has been caused or which can be tolerated. The implementation puts together the components we have developed:

$$
\text{OPT} \triangleq \text{OVAR} \parallel \underset{t\in T}{|\ |} (t : \text{TRANSACT} \parallel t : \text{FINAL} \parallel \underset{u\in T\backslash\{t\}}{|\ |} \text{NOINT}_{t,u})
$$

The generally accepted correctness criterion for maintaining the consistency of a database is called *serializability* [Papadimitriou, 1979]. A sequence of atomic reads and writes is called *serializable* essentially if its overall effect is as though the processes took turns, in some order, each executing their entire transaction indivisibly. The reader may be wondering how the optimistic transaction processing described above relates to this notion of serializability.

Define the function f_s for each trace s, which, when applied to transaction t returns the sequence of *reads* and *writes* performed by t in s:

$$
\text{f}_s\, t \triangleq s \upharpoonright \alpha(t : \text{VAR})
$$

Clearly, $f_s t$ is t's entire transaction in s. Now define the function *success* which, when applied to a trace s returns the sequence of names of successfully committed transactions:

$$
\text{success}\ s \triangleq \text{trans}^* (s \upharpoonright \bigcup_{t\in T} \text{Commit}_t)
$$

where *trans* merely projects the transaction name from an event:

$$\boxed{\text{trans t.e} = \text{t}}$$

Given a trace of *OPT*, *tr*, we can find the sequence of entire transactions, in the order of their successful commitment, as follows:

$$\boxed{\text{serial tr} \triangleq \text{ } \hat{} / (\text{f}_{\text{tr}}^* \text{ (success tr)})}$$

If *tr* is a trace of our optimistic transaction processing system, then *tr* and *serial tr* have the same effect. The proof of this fact follows from each transaction's view of the shared data and the freedom from interference that each successfully committed transaction enjoys.

5.5 PROOFS

Lest the reader think that we have forgotten to do our proofs, we present a short one in this section. We have started work on machine assistance for CSP proofs [Davies, 1987] using 'B', a program devised by Jean-Raymond Abrial [Abrial, 1986], and the following proof was developed with this system. Only a few of the proofs for systems in this chapter have been carried out in such a formal and detailed manner as the proof in this section. Most exist as paper and pencil exercises, carried as far as the author felt was necessary; they could all be formalised as this one has been.

Consider the following pair of predicates on traces:

$$\text{IN} = (\text{tr}{\downarrow}\text{l} = \text{tr}{\downarrow}\text{r} + 1) \qquad\qquad \textit{definition}$$
$$\text{OUT} = (\text{tr}{\downarrow}\text{l} = \text{tr}{\downarrow}\text{r}) \qquad\qquad \textit{definition}$$

These two predicates should have a familiar look about them; they form part of a theory of *bracketted actions* that we have constructed using 'B'. Now consider the following process:

$$\alpha\text{B} = \{\text{l}, \text{r}\} \qquad\qquad \textit{definition}$$
$$\text{B} = \mu\text{X} \cdot (\text{l} \longrightarrow \text{r} \longrightarrow \text{X}) \qquad\qquad \textit{definition}$$

This process, which alternates between its two events, should also be familiar. It is a theorem that B satisfies:

$$\text{BSPEC} = \text{IN} \vee \text{OUT} \qquad\qquad \textit{definition}$$

that is,

B sat BSPEC tr

The theory *bracket1* contains lemmas that are useful in the proof: *B* is guarded in *X*; and some simple theorems about *BSPEC*, *IN*, and *OUT*:

$$OUT^s_{tr} \wedge OUT^t_{tr} \Rightarrow OUT^{s\hat{\ }t}_{tr} \qquad\qquad L1$$

$$OUT^s_{tr} \wedge IN^t_{tr} \Rightarrow IN^{s\hat{\ }t}_{tr} \qquad\qquad L2$$

$$OUT^s_{tr} \wedge BSPEC^t_{tr} \Rightarrow BSPEC^{s\hat{\ }t}_{tr} \qquad\qquad L3$$

$$tr = \langle 1, r \rangle \Rightarrow OUT \qquad\qquad L4$$

$$tr \leq \langle 1, r \rangle \Rightarrow BSPEC \qquad\qquad L5$$

Another theory, *trace*, contains the theory of traces, whilst another, *satis*, contains the theory of processes satisfying their specifications, as set out in [Hoare, 1985]. We refer to these rules in the proof.

First we prove the basis for our induction.

$$
\begin{array}{lll}
1 & \text{STOP sat } tr = \langle\rangle & \text{satis.5} \\
  & \Rightarrow tr \leq \langle l, r \rangle & \leq.1 \\
  & BSPEC & L5
\end{array}
$$

Assuming the induction hypothesis:

2   X sat BSPEC

The proof of the induction step is as follows:

$$
\begin{array}{lll}
3 & (1 \longrightarrow r \longrightarrow X) \text{ sat } tr \leq \langle l, r \rangle \vee (\langle l, r \rangle \leq tr \wedge BSPEC^{tr''}_{tr}) & \text{sat.4c} \\
  & \Rightarrow tr \leq \langle l, r \rangle \vee (tr = \langle l, r \rangle\hat{\ }tr'' \wedge BSPEC^{tr''}_{tr}) & \text{head.3} \\
  & \Rightarrow tr \leq \langle l, r \rangle \vee (tr = \langle l, r \rangle\hat{\ }tr'' \wedge OUT^{\langle l, r \rangle}_{tr} \wedge BSPEC^{tr''}_{tr}) & L4 \\
  & \Rightarrow tr \leq \langle l, r \rangle \vee (tr = \langle l, r \rangle\hat{\ }tr'' \wedge BSPEC^{\langle l, r \rangle\hat{\ }tr''}_{tr}) & L3 \\
  & \Rightarrow tr \leq \langle l, r \rangle \vee BSPEC & \text{subst} \\
  & \Rightarrow BSPEC \vee BSPEC & L5 \\
  & \Rightarrow BSPEC &
\end{array}
$$

Thus we have shown both the basis and the inductive step, and since the process is guarded,

$$4 \quad \mu X \cdot (1 \longrightarrow r \longrightarrow X) \text{ sat BSPEC}$$

Q.E.D.

Many of the proofs of satisfaction can be automated in this way: the proof is performed first by hand, and then checked by the machine. Since many of the processes and their specifications are very similar, there have been many opportunities to structure and reuse proofs. However, it seems much more difficult to use a proof assistant such as 'B' to perform process transformations, since there is a rapid expansion in the number of terms in an expression. It seems that a special purpose tool is required to conduct such transformations, such as the occam transformation system [Goldsmith, 1987].

5.6   DISCUSSION

This chapter describes part of a very successful, but fairly primitive kind of system with which we are familiar. We have not described *robust* interfaces:

the systems can suffer certain deadlocks if processes do not obey the protocol required to use the shared data. However, there are well-known techniques that co-operative processes can employ to get round these problems, and we do not pursue the matter further (but see, for example [Ben-Ari, 1982] or [Raynal, 1986]). In the real-life system that we have been studying, locks are actually organised hierarchically.

The optimistic transaction processing system should be able to avoid these tiresome outcomes: transactions need not wait upon other transactions to finish before they can start. Of course, processes should be warned that the possibility of deadlock has been traded for the possibility of starvation.

The work of which this chapter is a part has started to show that CSP is a practical tool that may be used in industry. However, just like other formal methods that have been introduced into industry, such as Z [Hayes, 1987; Sufrin, 1986] or VDM [Jones, 1986], education is essential before any degree of fluency in using CSP is achieved, or even before a chapter such as this may be read. The use of CSP allows a designer the opportunity to specify systems in a concise fashion. For example, the optimistic transaction processing system has a very short and simple specification, even though it is a lot more sophisticated than the other systems considered, as is borne out by its design and implementation.

The style adopted in this chapter seems quite successful: specify each requirement separately, in the simplest context that seems appropriate; implement each requirement as a simple process; form the specification from the conjunction of requirements, and the implementation from the parallel combination of the processes. The development of two complementary descriptions – a predicate and a piece of process algebra – helped us to understand what we were describing much better than a single description would have done. Our confidence was bolstered by performing the usually simple proof that the process was indeed an implementation of the specification: that the two descriptions were of the same thing.

Many of the specifications and implementations in the systems that we have presented in this chapter are really the same predicates and processes in different guises. We could obtain an economy of expression by the widespread use of relabelling functions, but it is felt that this often leads to rather obscure descriptions. The first reaction of the reader is often to try to do all the substitutions in his head, to see what the definition really means. So we have limited such relabelling to situations where it is easy to see what is going on. For example, in promoting a property of a process to being a property of a labelled process, for any label in some set, relabelling is a powerful technique which actually makes it easier to understand the system. Drawing a rather tenuous link between disparate system properties, on the other hand, seems to obscure the issues. The insight about the connection is more valuable as a way of reducing the burden of proof than as a way of making the description more comprehensible. We will get the economy of an easy implementation and its proof, the strategy being merely to exhibit a relabelling scheme to establish the connection with an existing satisfaction proof.

The style of writing the predicate as a firing condition for an event was also helpful. Instead of writing rather complicated predicates – with plenty of existential quantifiers – which we *thought* captured a requirement, we wrote several smaller predicates describing firing conditions which matched our intuitions about the problem.

It would be a fairly straightforward matter to translate the CSP implementations of the systems that we have described into occam [inmos, 1984]. This would be a good idea because occam has direct language support for many of the concepts of CSP: it was designed with this in mind. It is also a simple language with relatively simple semantics; a proof of the translation would not be too difficult. For many reasons occam is not *yet* everyone's first choice for the implementation of concurrent systems. Companies have in-house standards: they support some languages and not others; they have concerns of compatibility, and of running systems on a large variety of different computers. We address ourselves elsewhere to the problems of implementing CSP descriptions in low-level languages with only meagre synchronisation facilities.

In this chapter we have omitted most of the proofs that we conducted in the development of each system. There are three sorts of proof that we have found: proofs of theorems about predicates over traces; proofs that processes satisfy their specifications; and proofs of equivalence between processes – process transformations. None of the proofs that we have carried out seems particularly difficult; however, they are often long and tedious, and we have made many a slip. Now that we understand how each proof may be made, we would like to check it with mechanical assistance, and we propose to conduct some research in this area. *Appropriate* mechanical assistance will have a large impact on the acceptance of a notation such as CSP in industry; we must get it right.

5.7 ACKNOWLEDGEMENTS

This work has been carried out under a contract with IBM United Kingdom Laboratories, Hursley Park, Winchester, to whom we are most grateful for their continuing support and interest. The problem of describing these kinds of transaction processing systems in the notations of CSP was suggested by Peter Lupton, who also made some very helpful comments on an earlier draft of this chapter, as did Geoff Barrett, Jeremy Jacob, and Steve King. The inclusion of a potentially more difficult system – using an optimistic strategy – was suggested by reading a description of the Amœba file service written in Z [Gleeson, 1986]. Paul Gardiner provided many important insights into this, and other, problems. Some elegant solutions to problems in transaction processing – developed independently and entirely in CSP process algebra, without trace specifications – may be found in [Arcus and Jacob, 1986].

Another approach using functional programming to produce some rather surprising results is being explored by John Hughes at Glasgow University, and Phil Trinder in Oxford. Jim Davies has formalised many of the proofs in this chapter using 'B' [Davies, 1987]. His work is only just beginning, but shows great potential. Anonymous referees gave some extremely useful comments on an earlier draft of the chapter. Finally, thanks – as usual – to Jock McDoowi.

5.8 REFERENCES

Abrial, J.-R. (1986) *The B User Manual*, First Draft, Oxford University Computing Laboratory, Programming Research Group.

Arcus, M. and Jacob, J. (1986) 'Flagship synchronisation problems in CSP', Industrial Software Engineering Unit, Report Number 1, Oxford University Computing Laboratory, Programming Research Group.

Ben-Ari, M. (1982) *Principles of Concurrent Programming*, Engelwood Cliffs: Prentice-Hall International.

Davies, J. (1987) 'Assisted Proofs for Communicating Sequential Processes', MSc Dissertation, Oxford University Computing Laboratory, Programming Research Group.

Gleeson, T. (1986) 'The Amœba File Service', The Distributed Computing Software Project, Oxford University Computing Laboratory, Programming Research Group.

Goldsmith, M. (1987) 'occam Transformation at Oxford', Oxford University Computing Laboratory, Programming Research Group.

Hayes, I., ed. (1987) *Specification Case Studies*, Englewood Cliffs: Prentice-Hall International.

Hoare, C. A. R. (1983) *Notes on Communicating Sequential Processes*, Technical Monograph PRG-33, Oxford University Computing Laboratory, Programming Research Group.

Hoare, C. A. R. (1985) *Communicating Sequential Processes*, Englewood Cliffs: Prentice-Hall International.

inmos ltd (1984) *occam Programming Manual*, Englewood Cliffs: Prentice-Hall International.

Jackson, M. A. (1983) *System Development*, Englewood Cliffs: Prentice-Hall International.

Jones, C. B. (1986) *Systematic Software Development Using VDM*, Englewood Cliffs: Prentice-Hall International.

Papadimitriou, C. H. (1979) 'The Serializability of Concurrent Database Updates', *Journal of the Association for Computing Machinery*, 26(4), 631–53.

Raynal, M. (1986) *Algorithms for Mutual Exclusion*, translated by D. Beeson, North Oxford Academic.

Sufrin, B. A., ed. (1986) *Notes for a Z Handbook*, Oxford University Computing Laboratory, Programming Research Group.

Woodcock, J. C. P. (1987) 'Transaction Processing Primitives and CSP', *IBM Journal of Research and Development*, 31(5), 535–45.

5.9 GLOSSARY OF SYMBOLS

This glossary of symbols is taken from [Hoare, 1985], except that we have
included substitution for free variables in predicates, and we do not require
relabelling functions to be injections, but find the definition given in [Hoare,
1983] to be more convenient.

5.9.1 Definitions

Notation	*Meaning*	*Example*
$\triangleq$	is equal to by definition	$R \triangleq \{\text{read.c} \mid c \in C\}$

5.9.2 Predicates

Notation	*Meaning*	*Example*
$=$	equals	$x = x$
$\neq$	is distinct from	$x \neq x + 1$
$P \wedge Q$	P and Q	$x \leq x + 1 \wedge x \neq x + 1$
$P \vee Q$	P or Q	$x \leq y \vee y \leq x$
$\neg P$	not P	$\neg 3 > 5$
$P \Rightarrow Q$	P implies Q	$x < y \Rightarrow x \leq y$
$P \equiv Q$	P if and only if Q	$x < y \equiv y > x$
$\exists x \in A \cdot P$	there exists an x in set A such that P	
$\forall x \in A \cdot P$	for all x in set A, P	
$P[a/b]$	P with a substituted for b	$(x < 9)[3/x] \equiv (3 < 9)$

5.9.3 Sets

Notation	*Meaning*	*Example*
$\in$	is a member of	$2 \in \{1, 2, 3\}$
$\notin$	is not a member of	$4 \notin \{1, 2, 3\}$
$\{a\}$	the singleton set containing a	$\{\text{start}\}$
$\{a, b, c\}$	the set with members a, b, and c	$\{\text{request, lock, unlock}\}$
$\{x \mid P\ x\}$	the set of all x such that P x	$\{\text{read.c} \mid c \in C\}$
$A \cup B$	A union B	$\{1\} \cup \{2, 3\} = \{1, 2, 3\}$
$A \setminus B$	A minus B	$\{1, 2, 3\} \setminus \{2\} = \{1, 3\}$
$\bigcup_{i \in I} S_i$	the union of a family of sets	

5.9.4 Functions

Notation	*Meaning*	*Example*
f x	function application, f of x	succ tr
$strip_l$	the function which removes the label l	$strip_t$ t.lock = lock
$strip_l^{-1}$	the function which adds the label l	$strip_t^{-1}$req = t.req
f^{-1} S	the inverse image under f of S	$strip_t^{-1}$ R =
		$\{t.read.c \mid c \in C\}$
$a \mapsto 1$	a maps to 1	$f \triangleq \{a \mapsto 1, b \mapsto 2\}$
$f \oplus g$	function override	$f \oplus \{a \mapsto 3\}$

5.9.5 Traces

Notation	*Meaning*	*Example*
$\langle\rangle$	the empty trace	
$\langle a \rangle$	the trace containing only a	$\langle t.commit \rangle$
$^\frown$	one trace followed by another	$\langle t \rangle^\frown s$
$^\frown/$	distributed catenation	$^\frown/\langle\langle a\rangle, \langle b, c\rangle\rangle = \langle a, b, c\rangle$
$s \upharpoonright A$	s restricted to A	$tr \upharpoonright W$
$s \leq t$	s is a prefix of t	$\langle a, b\rangle \leq \langle a, b, c\rangle$
$s \underline{\text{in}} t$	s is in t	$\langle b, c\rangle \underline{\text{in}} \langle a, b, c, d\rangle$
$s{\downarrow}a$	the number of as in s	$\langle a, a, b, a, c\rangle = 3$
s_0	the head of s	$\langle a, b, c\rangle_0 = a$
s'	the tail of s	$\langle a, b, c\rangle' = \langle b, c\rangle$
$\overline{s}$	the reverse of s	$\overline{\langle a, b, c\rangle} = \langle c, b, a\rangle$
$\overline{s}_0$	the last element of s	$\overline{\langle a, b, c\rangle}_0 = c$
$\overline{s}'_0$	the penultimate element of s	$\overline{\langle a, b, c\rangle}'_0 = b$
$f^* s$	f applied to every element of s	$f^* \langle a, b, c\rangle = \langle f\,a, f\,b, f\,c\rangle$

5.9.6 Events

Notation	*Meaning*	*Example*
l.a	participation in event a by process named l	t.lock
c.v	communication of value v on channel c	read.b
l.c.v	communication of value v on channel l.c	t.read.b

5.9.7 Processes

Notation	*Meaning*
αP	the alphabet of process P
$(a \longrightarrow P)$	a then P
$(a \longrightarrow P \mid b \longrightarrow Q)$	a then P choice b then Q
$(x : A \longrightarrow P\ x)$	choose x from A then P x
$\mu X \cdot F\ X$	the process X which satisfies $X = F\ X$
$P \parallel Q$	P in parallel with Q
$1 : P$	P with name 1
$P \square Q$	P choice Q
b!e	on channel b output the value of e
b?x	from channel b input to x
$f^{-1}\ P$	the inverse image under f of the process P
tr	an arbitrary trace of the specified process
ref	an arbitrary refusal of the specified process
P sat S	process P satisfies specification S

5.10 ADDITIONAL NOTATION

The notations used in this chapter are all drawn from [Hoare, 1983, 1985], with the following exceptions, which are either derived or are notational conveniences.

Given a sequence of events *s* containing an event *e*, then:

s before e

is the largest prefix of *s* not containing *e*. That is,

$\neg(\langle e \rangle\ \underline{in}\ (s\ \underline{before}\ e))$

and:

$(s\ \underline{before}\ e) \string^ \langle e \rangle \leq s \string^ \langle e \rangle$

Given a predicate on traces *PSPEC*,

1.PSPEC

denotes a new predicate that may be satisfied by a process named by *l*.

$$l.\text{PSPEC} \mathrel{\widehat{=}} \text{PSPEC}[\text{strip}_l^* \text{tr} \mathbin{/} \text{tr}]$$

In CSP we have the proof rule (taken from [Hoare, 1985], p. 91):

if P **sat** PSPEC
then f^{-1} P **sat** $\text{PSPEC}[f^* \text{ tr} \mathbin{/} \text{tr}]$

We can therefore derive the following proof rule:

if P **sat** PSPEC
then $l : \text{P}$ **sat** $l.\text{PSPEC}$

since:

$$l : \text{P} \mathrel{\widehat{=}} \text{strip}_l^{-1} \text{ P}$$

Also, since:

if P **sat** S
and Q **sat** T
then $(\text{P} \parallel \text{Q})$ **sat** $(\text{S}[\text{tr} \upharpoonright \alpha\text{P} \mathbin{/} \text{tr}] \wedge \text{T}[\text{tr} \upharpoonright \alpha\text{Q} \mathbin{/} \text{tr}])$

we can derive:

if P **sat** PSPEC
then $\displaystyle\parallel_{l \in L} l : \text{P}$ **sat** $\forall l \in \text{L} \cdot l.\text{PSPEC}$

Index

Index